BE A
LEADER

Be Who You Want To Be

Post Hill
PRESS

A POST HILL PRESS BOOK

ISBN: 978-1-64293-028-3
ISBN (eBook): 978-1-64293-029-0

Be A Leader:
Be Who You Want to Be
© 2018 by Nezha Alaoui
All Rights Reserved

Cover design by Cody Corcoran
Cover illustration by Ya Chin Chang

Post Hill Press, LLC
New York • Nashville
posthillpress.com

Published in the United States of America

To my inspiring daughters and my powerful Mayshad team.

CONTENTS

BE WHO YOU WANT TO BE

One of the hardest choices you will have to make in life is choosing to be yourself. To let go of the person you think you need to be, or what others expect you to achieve, and simply be who you want to be. Completely. Freely. Fearlessly. Ultimately, your destiny should be decided by you. Will you choose to stand for what you believe in, pursue what you love, and give yourself completely to what truly matters? You are the leader of your own life. The choice is yours and yours alone.

When I was a little girl, whenever anyone asked me what I wanted to be when I grew up, I would always answer with absolute certainty: "I want to be a businesswoman." My parents would challenge me and ask what I thought that meant.

"I want to run many businesses," I'd answer, "and I want to always be in airplanes." At seven years old, I may not have had the sophistication or vocabulary to articulate the vision I had for my future, but I knew that what I was going to build was going to be so fulfilling that it would be a lifestyle. As children, we are very intuitive, but as we are influenced by the expectations of our parents, school, and society, life reshapes our dreams, and we often end up settling for a lesser version of what we once instinctively knew we wanted.

I was born and raised in Morocco in an aristocratic family. My parents divorced when I was six years old. At the time, this was unheard of in our conservative society, but they bravely chose to pursue separate (but parallel) paths, rather than remain in an unhappy marriage and continue to live a lie for the sake of what was expected of them. When they sat me down with my older brother to announce their decision, I remember evaluating the situation and coming to the conclusion that our parents had the right to be happy.

Instead of feeling angry or sad, I made a choice to embrace the change. They still loved us and would always be there to care for us, so why be miserable and make them feel guilty for wanting to be true to themselves? My parents made sure to never express negative feelings for one another to us. When they both went on to remarry, we became a blended family with the addition of two beautiful sisters from my mom's side and two great brothers from my dad's side. By leading their lives with a balance of respect for both our and their individual happiness, they inspired me to always be true to myself.

School was never a great fit for me. I was bored and restless, which often got me into trouble (and eventually got me kicked out) because I was too creative and too dynamic for their rhythm. By my mid-twenties, I had learned to channel my innate drive and ambition into building a successful business in Morocco. I had a husband, two beautiful baby girls, twelve stores, and a life that was much more conformist than I wanted it to be. There's a fine line between being free and being lost. At some point, I realized that true freedom is giving direction to your life.

By society's standards, my life was successful. But, deep down, I knew I needed more than that. I was following a comfortable and safe path, but the vision of my life that I had had at seven years old was so much bigger than the life I was living. I knew that I had a larger purpose. I wanted my work and my mission to have a positive global impact. When I started traveling more for work, I began meeting people from all over the world who opened up to me about the struggles in their lives. I was always able to analyze what they were going through, simplify the issues, and find solutions. People would tell me all the time that I should become a therapist or a life coach. I realized then that I had a mission to help people, but I knew that as long as I stayed in my comfort zone, I would never really spread my message on a global level. So I decided to deconstruct my entire life and keep only what was essential: my daughters, who were a year and a half and three years old at the time.

I decided to embrace who I was and began building the life I had envisioned for myself as a young girl. I took my life apart and put it back together on my own terms. At the age of twenty-seven, I opened my first bank account on my own and became financially and emotionally independent. You can't imagine the freedom that comes with liberating yourself from other people's expectations. I started creating rules for my life and removing negativity from my relationships and my lifestyle.

For a long time, I was pleasing everyone in my life but myself. Then I finally arrived at a point where I decided that my daughters would be the only judges in my life. The only limit to my freedom: their wellbeing and happiness. My only duty: to be a happy and healthy mother. As long as they were smiling, I knew I was doing fine.

There were moments in this process of shaking things up in my life that were truly a struggle. I kept a pair of sneakers in the trunk of my car, and whenever my thoughts were charged with fear, guilt, doubt, frustration, or anger, I would go for a run to get my head straight before returning home to my daughters. With my heartbeat pounding to the rhythm of my playlist, I'd run as long as I needed to run, cry as long as I needed to cry, and scream as loud as I needed to scream. Then I went home to my children, unburdened by negativity.

In 2014, I started the Mayshad Foundation (named for my daughters, Maysoon and Shadeen), a nonprofit organization that develops and implements grassroots projects that focus on achieving sustainable development goals throughout marginalized African communities. As my vision began to crystallize into a philosophy of "Be Who You Want to Be," I founded MayshadMag.com, a global advocacy platform that brings together aspiring entrepreneurs and visionaries who can share inspiration and ideas through the empowering leadership movement: #BWYWB.

It is possible to live in harmonious balance between our wishes and our duties, without giving up on our dreams. I am an international entrepreneur who juggles her time between being a single mother of two inspiring daughters, running a team of motivated men and women, and working on exciting and fulfilling projects. I am living exactly the life I always wanted.

Sometimes, in our searching and need for acceptance, we lose sight of our dreams and grow deaf to our inner voice. Then, worn down by our madly stressful lives, there comes a point where we finally realize that the essence of fulfillment is based, above all, on a fundamental happiness that is not gained from social status or material possessions, but from a balanced life.

Leadership is a choice we make daily to live with positivity, gratitude, authenticity, and acceptance. To stop dreaming of greatness and dare to live it. To rise not just to our potential, but to also inspire others to embrace their own. There will always be opinions. There will always be expectations. Being a leader is running boldly towards the things we love instead of holding back for fear of failure. It's opening our hearts to the world and making others' needs our needs. It's having the courage to pursue the ideas we've kept inside and find our purpose in life. Above all, it's being able you look back on it all and knowing we have lived our lives on the terms that matter most—our own.

—Nezha Alaoui

CHAPTER 1

LEADERSHIP: A CONCEPT OR A REALITY?

There's a lot of talk about leadership in the world today. Success in any arena, from the classroom to the boardroom, is often measured by our ability to lead. But, what does it really mean to be a leader? At the most basic level, it is the act of guiding others towards achieving a common goal. The qualities of a leader vary from person to person. We all have the capacity to lead. The key is to identify your strengths and weaknesses, and to do this, you must go through a process of introspection.

To be an effective leader, we need to understand ourselves, and we need to understand life in general. We need to have the capacity to motivate ourselves, as well as to motivate others in the direction we want them to go. We must be innovative and have the courage to make choices with conviction. We must seek to understand who we are, whom we want to lead, and where we want to go. If we don't go through this process, we are addressing the concept of leadership, not the reality.

The most important trait in my personality—one that has allowed me to overcome my weaknesses and become the successful businesswoman I am today—is that throughout my life I have been an observer. As a child, my curiosity about the human condition was insatiable. I was constantly observing others and the world around me, trying to find the common threads inherent to all leaders, the common threads leading to happiness, and so on—which made me an odd child because I was questioning all these philosophical concepts at five years old. This sensitivity has allowed me to learn and keep learning, not only from my own experiences and mistakes, but also from those of others. As I matured and became a young mother at the age of twenty-four, I chose to put myself on a path to enlightenment and self-improvement. Through this journey, I acquire continuous wisdom by constantly seeking answers.

Leadership is not something that can be learned in a classroom. It is an art, a practical skill, and a way of life that we must internalize and practice every single day.

LET GO OF YOUR EGO

There is our true self, which is the essence of who we are—some call it our intellect, others call it our *soul*—and then there is our *ego*. Our ego is the other self inside of us who haunts our true self. The ego is our worst enemy because it fuels our worst impulses and disguises illusion as reality. When we learn to differentiate the ego from the self, we begin to recognize there are certain emotions that feed our ego, and those emotions are not a sustainable driving force.

For instance, when we buy an expensive watch or handbag, we subconsciously know that it represents a symbol of wealth or status to the people around us. There is a certain amount of pleasure that comes from others admiring or coveting these materialistic possessions. In other words, it feels good when someone complements our luxury brand bag or timepiece. But, is it our true self who feels good? No, it's our ego feeding on vanity and pride. Today, that feeling might satisfy our ego, but tomorrow it's going to be hungry again, and we will feel that seductive pull to acquire more and more. We become a slave to our ego by constantly feeing it, because the ego is insatiable.

A true leader must be able to differentiate between the ego and the self and make a choice: Which do I want to feed more, my *soul* or my *ego*? Do I want to grow and evolve as a person, or do I want to have a life based on feeding my ego? Do I want to take control of my ego, or do I want it to control me? To be a real leader, we need to get to the point where our motivation is no longer ego-driven. As long as our lives are oriented around our ego, we will never get to that stage of real leadership. This is why I talk about leadership as a concept or as a reality. If you are being led by your ego, you are not a true leader. It's just a concept. You can feed your ego and feel powerful, but it's not real. Yes, you may have the material wealth and the status that make you feel like a leader, but you're not really leading others in the right direction.

The most important part of learning to be a true leader is to first recognize and divorce ourselves from our ego so we can inspire others to move in the right direction. When I was younger, I was led by my ego. I used my ability to influence others to satisfy my most superficial impulses. For example, when I was a schoolgirl, if it was a beautiful day and I wanted to feel the sun on my skin instead of sitting in a dreary classroom, I would come up with concepts like, "What if *none* of us go to class? The teacher can't punish us all." I would rally my peers around my plan, and they would follow, but I wasn't leading them down the right path. I was motivated by what felt good in the moment, rather than what was for the good of those I was leading.

As I grew older and began my journey of introspection, I learned to identify the qualities that made me a strong leader and began using those skills to lead others in a positive direction. We cannot destroy our ego, but we can tame it. So, we must always be vigilant. When we are feeling most confident and in control, that is when we have to check ourselves. We must always measure the sincerity of our choices by asking: Is this a choice that is led by my true self, or is it a choice that is led by my ego?

The ego is constantly in us, hungering for validation, but when we do the hard work of introspection, it elevates us to a state of true leadership. When we have the humility to understand that our ego is something living within us that must be tamed, then we have freed ourselves from ego.

INNOVATION AND THE CREATIVE MIND

When we think of the word "innovation," what often comes to mind is technology or building a startup in Silicon Valley. When we think of the "creative mind," we think of artists or designers. But, anyone, whether they are in finance or fine arts, can train their creative mind to find innovative solutions. Innovation is a state of mind and a mechanism that you can develop over time.

I recognized this quality at a very early age and trained myself in the silliest innovations so that, as I matured, I already had the mindset to come up with more sophisticated innovations. I knew I was innovative because I could always come up with solutions. Whenever I would encounter an obstacle, I was the type of person who would dig and dig until I found a way around it. I always made the choice to look at things positively: If there is an obstacle, there is a solution. If there is no solution, that means the problem is not real and we must learn to control our emotional response to it and move on.

I also began teaching my daughters, Maysoon and Shadeen, to apply innovative solutions while they were very young. When they came to me with a problem, I never solved it for them. Instead, I trained them to find their own solutions using logic. If my youngest daughter, Shadeen, came to me in tears, I would ask her, "Why are you crying? Are you bleeding?" Right away, she would stop crying and check herself. "No." Then I would ask, "Are you hurt?" And she would say, with a little sniffle, "Yes." So, I would ask, "Are you *physically* hurt?" She would think for a moment and say, "No...but I'm still hurt." This was her little five-year-old mind developing logical thinking by defining her emotions.

Crying is a general concept, so define what you are crying about. "I'm crying because Maysoon won't give me back my book." I would encourage her to find a solution to the problem. Of course, her initial response was, "But there is *no* solution. She doesn't want to give me back my book." So, I would say, "There must be a solution. If there is a problem, there is a solution. Come back to me with two solutions. I'll help you pick one and we'll implement it together."

Innovation is simply finding a solution to a problem, obstacle, or challenge. We cannot expect to find innovative solutions in our professional lives if we have not first trained ourselves to find solutions in our everyday lives. And, those solutions are often hiding in plain sight; we just need to have the drive and the clarity to find them. Before we can start leading populations, we need to be able to find innovative solutions to the small problems in our own lives. Then we can begin applying them to the daily lives of millions of people.

CHOOSE OR LOSE

We live in a world that is constantly in motion. A leader must always be prepared to choose a direction or a course of action. It's like the concept of being in water. Imagine you are in the sea. There is always a current taking you one way or another, so you need to have that awareness of moving your feet to propel your body in the direction you want to go.

Life is like that. If we don't make a choice, life will take us in another direction, depending on the currents.

There are those who act decisively, and there are those who are paralyzed by indecision. When we're faced with a choice and we don't make one due to fear, what happens? The situation makes a choice for us, and we end up learning nothing from it. A leader makes choices, whether they are good or bad. If we make the wrong choice, we can learn from that mistake. Then, when we're faced with that situation again, we have acquired the experience to choose more wisely and to teach others not to fail.

CONVICTION OF PURPOSE

In today's world of smart phones, social media, and the 24-hour news cycle, it's almost impossible to escape the influence of the world around us—the things that we see and the things we don't see. This constant flow of imagery and information is like an aura floating around us at all times, and, if we are not careful, we will absorb the influence of others like a sponge. A leader must have the ability to stay true to his or her convictions, even in the face of uncertainty.

If we imagine life as a line on a graph, it's never a straight path. There are constant peaks and valleys (and thank God life is beautiful like that, because it would be very boring otherwise). When we are in those down moments—and those moments shouldn't discourage anyone because they are part of the process—those who are not really convinced of their goals, by the life they are leading, or by their choices, will give up on their dreams, projects, and so on. The work of the leader is to learn to steady those ups and downs by building emotional stability and to stay true to his or her convictions in the face of adversity.

In life, there will be points where it feels as though we are walking in darkness. Those who lead their lives with conviction know that the light will return at some point. They will keep walking because they have faith in themselves, in the direction they are heading, and in the conviction of their purpose. When we have conviction, we're not swayed or discouraged by something we know deep down to be temporary. We are not following a trend or being influenced by others. We have a sincere purpose that leads us to this path, and we will walk it in the light or in the darkness.

QUALITY CONTROL

Obstacles are a normal part of the human experience, and they are there for everyone. We may look at a successful life and think that person is happy 24/7, that he or she has never had to deal with pain or disadvantage, but this is an illusion borne of our own insecurities. Everyone encounters obstacles on their journey. When we start accepting that we can't avoid the ups and downs, that's when we start taking control of our lives.

The process of taking control begins with asking yourself two questions: *Who am I?* and *What are my abilities?* Are you a morning person or a night owl? Are you happy working behind a desk, or are you someone who likes be out in the field? Childhood and adolescence are about exploration of self. By the time we get to our twenties, we've been living with ourselves long enough that we know who we are. It's time to accept and embrace who we are so we can begin working on our weaknesses and improve them.

There is only one person whom you can control on this Earth, and that person is you. The weakest people I meet on my path are the ones who are so insecure they think being "in control" means controlling everything and everyone around them. These people are negative about their lives and, when they face a challenge, they feel they are being punished by life. They think they are the unluckiest people on earth, and that the people around them who are successful are leading charmed lives. This type of person is not prepared for challenges, and they are always in shock like children. Instead of using their creative mind to find a solution, they see themselves as victims. They move backwards instead of forward, and without having learned from the experience.

When we're not engaged in that quest of finding leadership in our lives, it's easier to judge others than it is to question ourselves. That is why we must always return to that core process of introspection. If we're aiming for leadership, we must always be asking ourselves the real questions: *Who am I? What can I do? What are my limitations? What is my message? Whom do we want to lead?*

MOTIVATION AS INSPIRATION

Motivation is the tool to "walking the walk." That's why we have to make sure we are driven by the right impulses. If our motivation is more about ourselves than the journey, we will run out of fuel long before we have reached our destination. Our purpose needs to transcend our own personal interests. The motivation that endures, and that will truly empower us and take us through trials and challenges, is one that serves the interests of others as well as our own.

As we go from one level to the next in our quest for leadership, we will face moments of doubt. If our motivation is tied to the needs of others, it will carry us through because we have a larger purpose. If our motivation is ego-driven, we will succumb to doubt and insecurity because what we want today might not be what we want tomorrow or in six months. But, when our motivation and our goals are tied to something that is greater than our own needs, it brings stability to our purpose, and then there will be no limit to what we can achieve.

LIVING IN BALANCE

I have a vision in my planning for the next six months ahead. I have a vision for a year, and a vision for the next five years. Every morning I wake up and subconsciously lead my day in balance of what I did the day before. Every month, I look ahead at my planning for the coming weeks and take stock of how well I have achieved what I validated on my schedule the month before. I am always questioning my choices and my actions. It's a continuous process of self-awareness and reflection, which allows me to live in balance.

Daily questioning is healthy. For instance, if yesterday I was invited to dinner with a friend and I indulged myself, today the mechanism of self-awareness will lead me to eat less because I had a heavy dinner the day before. This approach of balance can be applied to every aspect of our lives—from our moments of productivity to the time we give to ourselves, to our time that we give to others. If we have had an unproductive day today, then we make up for it tomorrow by being more focused and working a little harder. Maintaining a balanced lifestyle is living in the moment we're in, while simultaneously taking into account what came before and what lies ahead.

Guilt is one of the worst feelings we can have. It imprisons us and prevents us from moving forward. When we live our lives as part of a continuum of balance, rather than a series of isolated experiences, we can always recover from whatever extreme or excess we have experienced. We can stop beating ourselves up for what we did yesterday and focus on getting the most out of today.

GET IN THE TRENCHES

The best leaders are those who lead from the frontlines. They are out there in the line of fire, taking risks and exploring new territories, fully committed to their goals and confident in their purpose. Not only do they have the confidence to make hard decisions, they have the courage to take responsibility for their choices—whether that leads to success or failure. It takes courage to open doors and be the first one to enter when you have no idea what to expect on the other side.

When faced with challenges, we must ask ourselves, "What do I have to lose?" More often than not, we will find that what is holding us back is tied to our ego—our status in society or the opinions of others. These things are not a part of reality. They are illusions created by our ego. What we always have to gain is experience, which is a tangible tool that can help us on our path to success.

True leadership is about heading in the right direction and leading others there with you. On the path to leadership, positive results demand continuous work. We must give our best to succeed, and we must give it every day. When we understand this and join our path to others who are on the same journey in life, that is where powerful leadership begins.

CHAPTER 2

BUILD YOUR OWN
ECOSYSTEM

We begin life in the warmth and safety of our mother's womb. Once we are born, we enter the world of childhood, where we are encouraged to live in our imaginations—to have imaginary friends and play pretend. This is a healthy stage of life that allows us to perceive the world through innocent eyes as we focus on exploring ourselves and the world around us. Then we grow up, and the transition from the bubble of our imaginary world to the realities of life can often be a harsh process.

The transition from childhood to adulthood is about exiting that safe, protected bubble and merging with the real world. As we are introduced to the realities of life, we start encountering disappointment because things aren't as simple or as easy as they seemed when we were children. We begin perceiving the negativity of others and the pressures that society put on us.

We feel attacked by the outside world, so we react in one of two ways. One option is to cut off our sensitivity. This protects us from being hurt, but it also cuts us off from experiencing all the good feelings that life has to offer—sensations like excitement, passion, and love. It makes us feel stronger to cut off our sensitivity, but it's not real strength because, in reality, we are isolating ourselves from our emotions. Sensitivity is the mother of all creativity. By turning it off, we are cutting off our ability to innovate. We can absorb information, but we're incapable of creating anything useful out of it.

The other option is that we don't protect ourselves at all. We leave ourselves open and vulnerable to all outside influences. We are sensitive and creative, but we become the type of person that is constantly tortured. When we turn on the television and see negative news, it depresses us and makes us apathetic rather than inspiring us to take positive action. People disappoint us over and over again because we're not moving forward with the education of our experiences, and we become victims of the world.

Either way, we stop growing because we have allowed negativity to dictate how we lead our lives. Thankfully, there is another option: a third path that will allow us to start building a strong inner self as we pursue leadership in our lives.

In phase one, you separated your *ego* from your *self*. Now, it's time to start building your own ecosystem. One that is sane, healthy, and free of negativity. Your ecosystem must be centered around *you*, which is the only thing you can really control in your life. It's not a selfish act; it's an essential process of cleaning out everything negative in your life in order to protect that which is most important: your *self*.

Our ecosystem is our world within the world that separates us from the toxicity in life. This space includes the people we hang out with, our professional colleagues, and our family, as well as our passions and projects. Building an ecosystem gives us that space to keep our sensitivity and be creative, yet also be protected. It creates an enormous invisible shield around us because we have surrounded ourselves with positive relationships and with healthy people who share our vision.

"WHAT IS THE MANIFESTO OF MY ECOSYSTEM?"

The first step to creating our ecosystem is understanding who we are. What we want in life is constantly evolving, so in order to build our ecosystem, we need to begin by identifying what we *don't* want. What gives us anxiety? What (or who) is it throughout our day that triggers stress and inhibits our productivity?

When I observe that someone on my team at Mayshad is not performing well, I sit with him or her and I say, "Analyze your mission. What is it that is slowing you down and preventing you from achieving your goals?" Once we have identified the obstacle to their productivity, we can remove it from the equation. If we are working as a team, we each bring strengths and weaknesses to the table and can balance each other out. We don't have to do what we don't like because there are other people on the team who are capable. What doesn't make you happy can make someone else happy. That's the crazy positive thing about this world. We're all complementary. We complete each other.

As a working mother, what used to give me anxiety was the stress of doing homework with my kids. I carried the dread of it around with me all day like a weight on my back, which created stress at home and at work. Their father felt it was a mother's duty—he had no anxiety about it because he felt no responsibility for it. I felt stress going to meetings with their teachers because they would tell me that my kids were struggling with their homework. Then, one day, I had a breakthrough. I met with their teachers and told them, "*You* have to find a solution to help my kids." They tried to make me feel guilty, but I stayed firm. "I am paying this school to teach my kids," I told them. "I'm not a teacher. I am teaching my kids a love of reading, but that's as much as I can do. *You* have to find the solution." Then I called their father and told him that we were hiring a tutor and that I was no longer doing homework with the kids. I have much more important things to teach them: life skills and leadership skills. If I have an hour with my daughters in the evenings before bedtime, I want to spend it teaching them about life. Once I removed that anxiety from my life, not only did my daughter's homework skills improve (because the school provided extra help and the tutor gave them the support they needed), but I was more productive in my day because I didn't have the stress hanging over me, slowing down my productivity.

"WHAT ARE THE RULES OF MY ECOSYSTEM?"

With the courage to get to know ourselves and identify our triggers and stressors, we can now begin establishing a set of rules for how to conduct our lives without stress. We let go of people who disrespect us because we know who we are and we're strong enough to say, "I will not get into a conflict with you. There are seven billion people out there. You go your way and I'll go mine."

The rules of our ecosystem are unique to us, and they must always apply to ourselves as well as to others. For example, as part of my ecosystem, I have a cancellation rule. I used to be the type of person who felt guilty every time I had to cancel a meeting. It got to the point where I stopped committing to meetings because I was always worried about having to make changes to my schedule. I'm a busy single mother of two trying to run a business. My schedule is constantly in flux. So, I decided to remove that anxiety from my life by allowing myself to cancel without guilt. That's a rule in my life, and maybe my rules are crazy, but they apply to me as well as to others. I can cancel, but you can cancel on me too. It goes both ways.

Another rule I have in my ecosystem is that whenever someone in my life comes to me for advice, whether it's someone on my team, a friend, or family member, I always insist they also come prepared with two potential solutions. That doesn't mean I expect them to solve the issue on their own, but it sets the tone for a positive discussion. When people come to us with a problem just to complain, they're not in the right frame of mind to find a solution, and they don't even know it. Worse, they are now passing that negativity on to us. In order to put people in the right mindset, I force them (just as I do with my daughters) to exercise their minds by thinking through the problem so I can help them find a bigger and greater solution.

In our ecosystem, we accept our own needs as well as the needs of others. It's about creating a space that is free of toxicity. The limit to one's freedom is the wellbeing of others. As long as we are not harming anyone, you have the right to be whatever you want to be.

"HOW DO I COMMUNICATE THIS CHANGE TO PEOPLE IN MY LIFE?"

Once we have identified the rules of our ecosystem, we can begin the process of communicating to the people around us (our friends, our family, our significant others, etc.) that we are going through a positive change and that these new rules will be positive for them, as well. It's important we take this time to explain our rules to everyone in our life, and we have to understand that it will be harder with people from our past than it will be with newer relationships.

First, we begin with all the new people we have taken on in our lives. If we have a new client, we tell them this is who I am as a professional. If we're on a date, we communicate who we are as a romantic partner. This honesty and clarity is a critical component of the healthy relationships in our new ecosystem. When we try to adapt to others, all we're doing is selling a lie. It might be easier to project an image of what others want us to be, but, inevitably, this leads to disappointment because we took on things that we never really accepted.

When we start building healthy relationships with new people in our lives, we subconsciously begin gravitating towards these new people, and we may even begin avoiding certain people from our past because we are afraid they will not accept the changes we have made in our lives. These people are the hardest to face, but, at some point, we need to get over that fear and communicate to them that we are going through a positive change. Trust me. They will be happier to find out about our new rules, rather than having us disappear from their lives.

It can be hard for the people we have known for a long time to accept the changes we are going through. They may be resistant because they think they are going to lose us in this transformation, so it's critical to explain that our motivation is not personal to them, but related to our own journey. Once we make them understand that they're not going to lose us and they will still be part of our change, they may even be inspired to make the some positive changes in their own lives.

"HOW DO I KEEP NEGATIVITY OUT OF MY ECOSYSTEM?"

As much as we would like to remove *all* toxicity from our lives, the reality is that there are people we interact with throughout the course of our daily lives that we simply can't avoid—from competitive coworkers and passive-aggressive family members to angry cab drivers and self-absorbed social acquaintances. The best way to deal with toxic people is with compassion and distance. If someone tries to draw us into a conflict, we can either get pulled into their toxic energy and space, or we can choose to rise above their negativity. When someone is pushing our buttons, we need to have the emotional distance to be aware that it's happening so we can begin to establish boundaries for when and where we interact with this person.

The best way to manage negative people is with compassion. When we respond to toxicity with anger and frustration, we allow ourselves to be pulled into someone else's conflict and, as a result, we surrender control. Anger pollutes our ecosystem and keeps us from peace and inspiration. Desire for revenge keeps us from moving on from a negative situation. Regret keeps us from learning from the experience. Compassion frees us from all that negativity and gives us the emotional clarity to established boundaries.

There are some friends or family members that we really love, but whom we can only spend so much time with before it becomes toxic. We don't have to cut those people off completely; we just need to learn to recognize how much exposure is toxic and set limits. Maybe we can only see those people in certain environments (like work or a yoga class), and maybe it can only happen once a week for an hour. By establishing the right amount of distance, we protect our ecosystem from being infected by other people's negativity.

Then there are people out there who I call "energy vampires." These are the worst kind of negative people because they are so toxic and self-absorbed they actually feed on our positive energy. Our energy is our biggest asset. We are waking up every morning and trying to work on ourselves and make positive changes in our lives. That process requires a lot of energy and hard work, so there is no room in our ecosystem for energy vampires.

OUR WORLD WITHIN THE WORLD

Our ecosystem is a solar aura that attracts positivity, opportunity, and achievement. This aura begins with *you* and grows through every one of your accomplishments. Every experience is an occasion to grow and get to the next level in our journey towards leadership. When we achieve great things, we look back and realize that even seemingly meaningless lessons have contributed to our present life.

CHAPTER 3

PROJECTION: A 5-YEAR PLAN TO YOUR DESTINY

Projection is about building a detailed vision of *where* we want to be and *who* we want to be. This is one of my favorite leadership exercises because it's the process by which we transform our dreams into a vision. The exercise is to imagine where we want to be on this day and at this time five years into the future, and then to project ourselves into that life. We do this at the beginning of building our vision, and then again any time we feel doubt about our direction.

Without projection, we can't know where we're heading. It's like hiring someone without a job description. You can hire the best expert in the world, but if you don't tell him what his mission is and what you expect from him, how can he do his job properly? We need to define our goals in order to build the life we want. I chose five years for this exercise for a specific reason. Projecting three years into the future is too close. In three years, we won't be significantly different from who we are now. This will block our imagination and unconsciously limit our dreams. Projecting ten years into the future is going to make us lazy. We're not going to do the exercise properly because we are too far removed from the person we will become.

Five years is the ideal distance for our vision. It's far enough into the future to imagine all the possibilities, but close enough to feel real and achievable. It's not just that we're going to be five years older. In reality, those five years are 1,825 days of hard work and opportunity that will become the roadmap to your destiny.

Transforming our dreams into a coherent vision begins with writing down in a journal where we are going to be in five years' time. It can be anywhere in the world that is related to a day in the life that we are going to be leading. A critical component of this exercise is that we write everything down. I have a collection of notebooks going back ten years to when I first began building my vision. If our vision exists solely in our imagination, it will be as fleeting and as unattainable as a dream. Writing things down gives our vision permanence by bringing it out of our minds and into the real world.

FOCUS ON THE DETAILS

When I do this projection exercise in my leadership workshops with college students, I'll often hear things like, "I want to be successful in five years," or "In five years, I want to be a billionaire." Yes, we all want to be successful (and who doesn't want to be a billionaire?), but those kinds of projections are too broad. They won't lead us anywhere. If we project ourselves without doing the work of constructing a detailed vision, the result will be vague. In order to transform our dreams into an achievable vision, our projection needs to be built on a solid foundation. We have to know the details of what we want our lives to be.

Once we have projected into a day five years into the future, we start imagining the rhythm of our day, beginning with our morning. What time do you wake up? Do you work out first thing to get your energy flowing, or do you take time for quiet contemplation? Do you wake up at 6:00 a.m. and head to the office, or do you sleep till 11:00 because you are at your most creative at 3:00 a.m.? *When* and *how* do you perform best? We have to respect our rhythm and construct our vision around it.

Now, *where* are you? Are you on a plane between meetings on two continents? Are you somewhere in the mountains, completely detached from the world, working on your novel? Are you sitting in a corner office, or are you traveling the world with a backpack? What is your home going to be? What is your office like? Imagine it. Design it. Next, populate your vision. Who are the people in your life? Even the ones you haven't met yet. Design them, as well. Be specific about what you want. There are seven billion people out there; if you know what you want, you'll find the people you're looking for. Do you want a husband or wife? What is that person like? Is he a Chinese businessman? Is she a bohemian artist? If all you know is that you want to be married, you'll end up either not married or (worse) you might end up married to the wrong person. But, if you know specifically what you're looking for in a life partner, then you'll recognize that person when you meet him or her.

Now that you have projected yourself in detail into a specific day and rhythm, the next step is to start imagining your life. How have you come to be where you are? Why are you on that mountain, writing that book? Where were you before you got on that plane, and where are you heading? You start digging deeper. Are you at a point in your life where you want to be settled down and starting a family, or do you want to be focused on your career? You start putting components into your projection that are related to your lifestyle, and you start designing the life you want. Then you start challenging your own ideas. Do all these components fit together? If not, what do I need to change?

I have designed exactly the life I wanted, and I am living it every single day. I do that by regularly constructing a detailed vision of my life built around a healthy respect for my personal rhythm. Since the age of sixteen, I have understood that I am the type of person who needs to be constantly in motion. If I stay more than one month in the same place, I'm not going to be productive. Travel energizes me. People ask me all the time, "How do you do it, Nezha? How do you cope with the constant jet lag and living out of a suitcase?" My answer is always the same: This is what gives me the positive power to achieve my goals.

Maybe you're like me, and all your life, you've been struggling because you couldn't fit into a rhythm that someone else had designed for you. Well, this is your opportunity to free yourself and build a life according to who you truly are. I was a hyperactive kid. School was too slow for me. Once I reached my twenties, I began to understand and embrace my own rhythm. I always have multiple projects going because I cannot do just one thing. If I do one thing, I will fail at it. If I do ten things, I will succeed at all ten.

Knowing what we want in life will allow us to recognize all the opportunities on our path. By the same token, when other people meet us and become a part of our lives, they will know how to help us achieve our goals.

DON'T BE AFRAID TO DREAM BIG

When I tell people to do this projection exercise, the first thing that often happens is they get shy about sharing their dreams. Without dreams, there is no vision. Without dreams, there is no passion and there is no conviction. When we do this exercise, we do it knowing we are trying to exceed our expectations and aspire to greatness. Don't set limits. The beauty of dreams is that the bigger they are, the more we can achieve.

Belong to the world. Don't put physical limits on where you are or who you want to be. Don't be scared to dream about another land. My own dream was to work for the United Nations in different parts of Africa, and I achieved it. In today's world, we can choose to be anywhere. Just a few generations ago, we were limited to certain geographical locations or industries—if you grew up in a small town and your father worked in a factory, that was going to be your path, as well. Today, the sky's the limit. Don't be scared to dream about a life that is very different from the one you grew up in. If, deep down, your dream is that you want to live in Japan, then that's your projection.

MAKE A DATE WITH YOUR CALENDAR

Now that we have constructed a detailed vision of who we are and where we are going to be in five years, it's time to focus on the year ahead. To achieve our vision, we need to get in touch with our calendar in order to be more organized in our daily thinking and in our annual strategizing. Time passes fast; if we don't have a plan for how to spend it wisely, then we're not in control of our time—time is controlling us.

Divide the calendar into three seasons of goal setting:

1. January – May
2. June – August
3. September – December

The first season is about giving ourselves goals in what I like to call the Three Bodies: the physical body, the intellectual body, and the spiritual body. We define what we need to work on in the coming year in order to make positive changes in these three critical parts of life.

Working on our physical bodies is about implementing healthy choices that make us look and feel better. Maybe we decide to take vitamins for our bones or to make positive changes to our diet. Our goals can be anything from changing our workout to taking the time to get a haircut.

Every year, we should be learning new things, so working on our intellectual body is about feeding our minds with information. Maybe this is the year we start learning a new language or get a little training in Photoshop.

Setting goals for our spiritual bodies is about identifying and taking action on the things that will make us happier and make other people happier when they are around us. Maybe we carve out a little more time for meditation, or maybe we resolve to gossip less and be more compassionate.

The second season of goal setting falls during the summer months, a time when things tend to slow down. So, June through August is our homework season. What do we need to catch up on to have a powerful September? Maybe that means spending quality time with our friends and family. This is the ideal time to recharge our batteries, because the third season of goal setting is all about taking action. If we've been feeling stagnant in our careers, this is the opportune time to start thinking about transition and how to effectively execute change. As August comes to a close, we begin planning our third season so we are fully prepared to take action on our goals.

We want to finish our summer with an actionable plan because September to December is a season of endless opportunity. This is the most productive period across all industries; it's when all the budgets are being negotiated for the following year. This is when we can pick up new clients, find a new job, get sponsors, or make our sales. This is the season when we must take action on our goals for the year, because by January, most industries are focused on implementing vision and budgets have already been allocated.

Keep in mind that this is a time of the year that passes quickly because midway through December, companies are winding down for New Year, and a lot of businesses shut down for two weeks. But, if we've done that end-of-August exercise and we've worked hard towards our goals for that fall season, we will arrive at the end of our year with so much joy and happiness. Now, it's time to rest and recharge again for January's goals.

Don't be afraid to readjust your strategy along the way. During the last week of every month, we review what we've set out as our goals for the coming months and assess our planning. Have we achieved our goals for the season? If not, we tweak and make adjustments according to what needs to be done. Then, every ten days, we plan our week ahead. Organization and careful planning are the keys to a stress-free and successful life.

CHAPTER 4

EMOTIONAL INTELLIGENCE: AN ASSET TO INVEST IN

When I was twelve years old, IQ tests were all the rage. I remember hearing a lot about this scientific measure of human intelligence that was supposed to quantify an individual's capacity for success in life. These tests measured your reasoning and problem solving skills, which was something that (according to the test-makers) you cannot grow or improve. IQ tests became so popular that employers and schools started using them as a method of screening for the best and brightest candidates.

My parents had a book on IQ in their library. So, one day, I decided to take the test and see for myself what all the fuss was about. My scores were terrible. Did this mean I would never be successful in life? How unfair would it be, I thought, if some people were born with the right genes for success while others were not? If it's all set in stone, why should anyone work hard in life? By that logic, the person blessed to be born with a high IQ can sit back and take life for granted because success is guaranteed, and I should just give up because, with my low score, I would never be able to achieve success.

Fortunately, I wasn't discouraged back then because I instinctively knew I had a different kind of intelligence that wasn't reflected in the test. I was perceptive, intuitive, self-aware, empathetic—qualities that made me the kind of teenager who was able to navigate between all the different social cliques without becoming trapped in any of their hierarchies. So, I came to the conclusion that there must be another way to measure success and leadership in life. Years later, when I was in my twenties, I started reading books on Emotional

Intelligence, and I realized that this was what I had been exploring since the age of twelve.

IQ VS. EQ

The IQ is one's ability to learn, understand, and apply information to skills. It measures things like logical reasoning, word comprehension, math skills, abstract and spatial thinking, and one's ability to filter out irrelevant information. The EQ (also known as Emotional Intelligence) is the ability to control, identify, and assess our own emotions, as well as those of others. While the IQ is a finite measure that cannot be improved, our EQ is something we can train and grow.

When Emotional Intelligence first came to popularity in the 1990s, it became the missing link that explained why people with average IQs outperformed those with the highest IQs 70 percent of the time. It completely debunked the idea that the IQ was the sole source of success, and decades of research now point to Emotional Intelligence as the most important component.

The beauty of Emotional Intelligence is that it gives people control of their destiny. Success in any realm is first and foremost a matter of choice, and with consistent work, anyone can achieve it. The question becomes: How do we grow and train our Emotional Intelligence on our path to leadership?

IDENTIFYING POSITIVITY IN YOUR LIFE

Emotional Intelligence is what gives us the strength to put distance between ourselves and negative situations. Growing our EQ begins with the exercise of looking for positivity in our lives. By responding to a situation with positivity, we control the impact of negativity, and, in turn, attract more positivity into our lives.

Two skills are critical to this exercise:

- Self-Awareness – The ability to accurately perceive our emotions and stay aware of them as they happen.
- Self-Management – The ability to use awareness of our emotions to stay flexible and to positively direct our behavior.

As leaders, we must learn to control our emotions and our thoughts in order to steer them away from of negativity, and we must direct our spirit and our mind into absorbing positivity from the world.

Positivity has nothing to do with material possessions. On my travels through Africa for the United Nations, I often encountered people who lived the most minimal existence, and yet exuded an aura of positivity. On one of these trips, I remember seeing an old man sitting on the ground, carving little figurines out of wood to sell to travelers. He was singing a happy tune and carving away. He had such a warm and inviting spirit that he had a line of people in front of him wanting to buy his little wooden figurines—not because they felt sorry for him, but because they were attracted to his positivity. I have no idea what this man would have scored on an IQ test, but I guarantee you his Emotional Intelligence was off the charts!

NEVER TAKE ANYTHING IN LIFE FOR GRANTED

This exercise is about practicing the art of gratitude. We must recognize, embrace, and be grateful for all the positive things we have in our lives, starting with the simplest and most basic. The gift of our five senses. The blessing that we are breathing and in good health. We have things until we stop having them, so enjoy them and be grateful for them on a daily basis.

The minute we start taking things for granted—whether it is an object, a skill, a person in our lives, or even our own bodies—that's the minute when we start deteriorating. Imagine if we said, "My body is my body and it will always be this way, so I don't have to invest in taking care of it with exercise or eating right." If we don't take care of our bodies, they begin to fall apart. The same goes for knowledge. If I thought that I owned leadership by publishing this book, then I would lose everything I ever worked for to get to where I am today.

MANAGE ENERGY SPENDING

Emotional intelligence is about observing ourselves and defining the things that help us build positive energy, as well as identifying the things that could potentially drain our energy.

We begin by making a list of all the things throughout our day that give us positive energy, from our workout or yoga class to that ice cream we treat ourselves to in the afternoon, and from reading books with empowering content to spending positive time with friends. Whenever we feel low in our energy, these activities will help us replenish our stores.

We work hard to grow our energy. It's our strongest asset, so we must learn to spend it wisely. Imagine that we have a checkbook, and every time we waste our energy negatively, we write a check. When we are faced with negativity in our lives, whether it's a conflict or a challenge, we can choose to write a one hundred-thousand-dollar check to deal with that situation. Where does that leave us?

Depleted.

Or, we can learn to control our energy spending by understanding that some situations are not worth the negative toll. Then, what could have cost us one hundred thousand dollars, will only cost us one thousand dollars because we have minimized the amount of energy we are willing to spend on that situation.

Once we have mastered controlling our energy spending, we will see that energy bill coming and we'll have the strength to say, "I'm not writing this check because it's not worth the energy it will cost me."

FIND WHERE YOU BELONG

The Emotionally Intelligent person who has grown a positive mindset will instinctively make choices that put us in situations and places where we fit. In life, we can't be great at everything, so the people who continually put themselves into situations where they're not able to perform at their best will never grow beyond a certain level.

I knew very early on that I did not have an aptitude for finance or science. Instinctively, I directed myself towards what I was good at: creativity. I began my journey as an artist. Once I found myself in a place where I fit, not only did my creativity blossom, but, little by little, I also found the confidence to begin growing my skills in finance and science, as well. That feeling of belonging to a creative world gave me the confidence to approach unfamiliar worlds without fear because I wasn't looking for a sense of belonging there.

We can reach out to everything in the world, but it starts with finding the place where we fit. When we are grounded in a sense of belonging, the things that once seemed complicated and unattainable will eventually move to within our reach. A sculptor may never become a tech whiz, but they will have the confidence to aspire to feeding that side of their intellectual curiosity.

We all need to feel we belong to something, that we fit somewhere in the world. This is the core of empowerment. Once we start experiencing that profound sense of belonging, it becomes like a beacon lighting our path and directing our journey of growth.

CHAPTER 5

WHERE DOES SPIRITUALITY STAND ON LEADERSHIP?

On my travels around the world, I have encountered so many people searching for spirituality in their lives. But, what is "spirituality?" And where does it come into play on the path to leadership? Spirituality is faith in life. Spirituality is our connection to the *self*. It's beyond the rituals and dogma of religious institutions. It's about connecting to the force of nature and the essence of creation. It's that key component that allows us to separate the *ego* from the *self*.

With time, consistency, and effort, we can achieve whatever we aim for in life. Dwelling in doubt, our moments of distraction, and our connection to the materialistic aspects of our goals all stop us from reaching our full potential and realizing our goals. Spirituality is that deepest layer of inner strength that gives us the ability to distance ourselves from negative situations and overcome obstacles and challenges. It's that core strength that we tap into on our path to leadership that allows us to tame our ego. The true practice of leadership originates within our inner spirituality, which keeps our focus directed towards goals that are beyond our immediate materialistic needs or ambitions.

True spirituality unclutters our minds, allowing for clarity of purpose. When we are faced with challenges, we accept that they are there for a reason. We recognize that an obstacle is an opportunity to improve our skills or adjust our strategy. Everything becomes an occasion for learning and a chance to grow.

The greatest leaders in history had strong spiritual beliefs. Nelson Mandela went to prison for his convictions, but never succumbed to negativity because he accepted that it was part of his spiritual journey. When we link to spirituality, our freedom is about being who we want to be. Whether we are caged in a room or feel trapped in a bad situation, we can find our own freedom regardless of the restrictions. Little by little, we start pushing the limits and, subsequently, expanding our frontiers.

Spirituality is food for the soul. We nourish our physical bodies with food, exercise, relaxation, and moments of pleasure. We nourish our intellectual body with knowledge. Too often, we neglect our spiritual body, which is the core and source of our energy. Nourishing the soul builds inner strength. For me, practices such as yoga, meditation, hiking in nature, and reading empowering books are ways to link myself to spirituality.

THE SPIRITUAL PILGRIMAGE

Finding spirituality in a world that is so busy and complicated can seem impossible. From the moment we open our eyes in the morning, we are greeted by overflowing email inboxes, unanswered text threads, and a constant barrage of news alerts and updates. To connect with our inner self, it is critical that we silence the noise. The best way to do to this is to make a spiritual pilgrimage.

The most spiritual pilgrimage is done in wild nature. It's a solitary experience, away from the crowds and insanity of modern life. Facing the immensity of nature allows us to enjoy the silence of life. The silence of nothing. In nature, there is nothing to consume, which in itself can be stressful because there are no distractions—no television, no social media, no stores from which to purchase anything. There's no escape. We have no choice but to listen to our own thoughts. Technology is simply a distraction, a means to escape the *self.* So, the feeling of being in nature is really encountering our *self* and our *soul* in their purest forms.

My own spiritual journey began in the desert. I have published books of my photography from my travels in the desert. This is what feeds my soul. The first time I found myself overwhelmed by the beauty and immensity of nature was in 2011, during my last mission for the United Nations. I was working with the World Food Program, visiting a refugee camp in Mauritania, on the border with Senegal.

I saw things there that I had never seen before. On the road to the refugee camp, we encountered a donkey dying of dehydration. It was barely breathing, its body so desiccated that it looked like a dried fruit or pressed flower. I was moved by both the beauty and horror of it. One couldn't help but look at this poor creature and feel humbled by the fragility of life. It seemed a fitting metaphor for what awaited me at the camp.

Even though it was October, the heat at midday was around 122 °F, so we spent the mornings visiting refugee camps, and by 2:00 in the afternoon, I would retreat to my small hotel to escape the scorching sun. We're talking about the kind of hotel that provided one towel for the week. No luxury. The manager, who was the nephew of the owner, remains a dear friend to this day. At night, he would put a carpet on the ground outside my room for me to sit on. He would pour water onto the plants around me to create a little humidity because the temperature outside was still around 104 °F, even after sunset. At that point in my life, I was going through a positive change of freeing myself from the pressures and expectations of society, and those moments in the solitude of the desert filled me up with the strength to face what I needed to face in my personal life.

Since then, I have been going on annual spiritual retreats to different deserts around the world. Whether I'm in India, Morocco, Mauritania, India, or Utah, these experiences feed my soul. In the desert, I am faced with the power of natural creation, which puts me in two states. First of all, I experience humility in the face of the immensity of what nature can create. It's a feeling of total insignificance, but, at the same time, such enormous power because the same immense force that created this vast and ancient landscape is within all of us. We can't help but ask ourselves, "Who am *I* in all of this?"

When we surrender to nature, we realize how blessed we are to be alive and to be a part of the universe. As a result, we start recognizing the power we have. And, we experience gratitude, which is an essential component of identifying positivity in our lives.

CONTEMPORARY MEDITATION

I'm the type of person who wakes up with a thousand ideas rushing through her mind. I'm a hyperactive person, always thinking and moving and creating. The idea of meditation used to seem utterly inaccessible, unrealistic, and incongruous with the reality of my daily life.

Then I realized that meditation doesn't have to be about going on a yoga retreat or being in a silent room and taking an hour a day to think about nothing. Meditation is not limited to that conformist format anymore. That may work for some, but I am definitely not that kind of person. I'm not spiritual in that way. My philosophy on the link between spirituality and meditation is much more contemporary. It's an approach that is more realistic and achievable for people in their daily lives.

A moment of meditation is simply a moment of rest for your mind. How we achieve those moments of rest is unique to every individual. For some, it could mean going for a walk or a run at the end of a stressful day. For others (like me) it could be working out with an empowering playlist that puts me in a positive mood. It could be that moment in the morning when we sit quietly and enjoy a cup of coffee or tea before our busy day begins. The method is up to the individual; the important thing is that it is a moment that generates peace and positivity in your day.

No matter where I am in the world, I always have an empowering book in my bag. It makes me feel safe because in moments of stress, I can pull out my book and quiet my mind by reading. The kinds of books I gravitate to can be very different, but there is always a fundament thread of empowering content.

There's a reason religions instruct us to read the Bible, the Torah, or the Koran every day. There is something sacred and spiritual that comes from the process of absorbing wisdom through the written word—books that nourish our spirit by giving us information we can use to empower ourselves. Reading empowering books in moments of stress reduces our anxiety by shifting us into a positive reality.

SPIRITUAL CONFIDENCE

Linking to spirituality is what helps us build a true and positive confidence that detaches us from externalism. Spiritual confidence is something that I turn to time and time again in my own life when I am faced with moments of doubt and frustration.

Recently, I was scheduled to speak at a high-profile conference in New York. It was going to be an important event for me on many levels, from networking and media exposure to making business contacts. Then, on the same day, I was invited to a very small conference in Paris where a woman who is a leader in education was speaking. This woman is so inspiring to me that I made the choice to cancel my own speaking engagement to attend this conference, instead. On the morning she was to speak, I arrived a half an hour early so I wouldn't miss a word of her speech—or so I thought. As I walked in, everyone else was leaving. It turned out I had mixed up the times and had just missed her talk. You can imagine how I felt in that moment. I had given up a significant speaking engagement of my own to listen to the words of another speaker who is very inspiring to me, and now I had missed out on both opportunities. It was potentially devastating because the consequences were both financial and spiritual.

This is where my spiritual confidence comes out. First of all, I know I can't blame anyone. I alone am responsible for my choices, and I accept the consequences of those choices. Second, I have a huge faith in life that nothing can shake. There is a reason why this happened. I just wasn't supposed to be there. I don't know what that reason is, and I never will know, but I accept it on faith and move on. There is nothing I can do to change what happened. I can't go back. I have to move forward. Instead of wallowing in disappointment and regret (which are pointless and paralyzing emotional reactions to situations we cannot control), I left that conference and ended up having a very productive day.

Spiritual confidence allows us to let go and accept irreversible situations beyond our control. It is an extremely important component to integrate into our lives on the path to leadership because the reality of life is that not everything goes the way we want or expect it to go. True spirituality gives us the confidence as a leader to adapt our vision when faced with challenges and to overcome any obstacle.

CHAPTER 6

CONFIDENCE: NURTURE A SEED INTO A POWERFUL TREE

When we think of the word "confidence," we often equate it with success, or we conjure the image of someone commanding a room with authority. True confidence is much more complex and multilayered than an appearance or a result. On the path to leadership, confidence is about how we relate to others, how we relate to our lives, and how we relate to our inner self. In other words, it's in the positivity we project and attract, in the knowledge and experience we acquire, and in a deeply rooted sense of self that grounds us in moments of true crisis.

We have already discussed the importance of differentiating the ego from the self. There is no confidence when we are ruled by our ego. Like a balloon that grows with air inside of us, as we feed our ego, it takes up space and gives us the impression that we are full of something. But, in truth, there is an emptiness inside we can't define. We've all encountered people with inflated egos who are puffed up by the appearance of success. These people are easily shaken when they don't get enough attention or are faced with difficult challenges because they are dependent on the materialistic aspects of life to make them feel respected and self-assured.

Confidence that is bound to our inner self is just the opposite. It fills us with contentment and peace and empowers our vision with truth and fairness. Think of it like a seed we can nurture within ourselves until it becomes a powerful oak that reaches for the light, bends with the currents of the wind, and stays firmly rooted through the harshest storms.

THE LEAVES

The first layer of confidence is what we communicate to others. It's the positivity we project to the world: our aura, our smile, and our conviction in the story we tell. It's the crown of leaves radiating from the tree, absorbing sunlight and transmitting life-giving oxygen back into the world.

This is the confidence that attracts positivity into our lives. People will be drawn to us because they want to be around someone who is convinced of who she is and what she has to share. Imagine you are out for a walk, looking for a place to eat dinner. You pass by two restaurants, one next to the other. The first is full of light, and music is emanating from inside. Through the windows, you see people smiling and enjoying themselves. The second restaurant is dimly lit, quiet, with only a few people sitting inside who don't seem very happy. Obviously, you are going to choose the first restaurant over the second because positivity attracts positivity.

THE TRUNK

The middle layer of confidence is our capacity to achieve what we are communicating to others. Just as the trunk gives a tree its strength and channels energy from its leaves to its roots, this layer of confidence connects our ideas to knowledge and nourishes them with experience. It's what gives us the ability to sustain our vision because our passion will be built on a solid foundation.

In order to build a consistent presence in an industry or community, we need to be coherent in what we are projecting to the world. We can be that joyful, positive person who has the ability to communicate our vision to others, but if we're selling a product or an idea without substance, we're not going to be able to sustain true relationships. We end up being the type of person who keeps moving from one place to another, one job to another, one circle of friends to another, because our inability to back up what we're communicating catches up with us and we are always having to find a new story to tell.

Picture yourself communicating to a group of people about your vision. Everyone is smiling and hanging on your every word. Now, go beyond the smiling faces and the people who are captivated by your words to that one person in the group who challenges your ideas because he or she is either a competitor, envious of you, or simply an expert in what you're talking about and questions your reasoning. Can you stand your ground, or do you back down? When confronted by opposition, the person who doesn't have knowledge and experience totally loses confidence.

I have always felt at ease when speaking in public about my vision of leadership and empowerment. The first time I was interviewed on television, I was surprised to find I wasn't nervous at all. It felt natural. It was just common sense for me. It was only years later, when I began to sit in on media training sessions, that I learned the reason I do not feel stress when speaking about my ideas (whether it's to a small group of students in a workshop or in front of a camera on national television) is because what I'm saying is connected to an inner truth. I'm not making it up on the fly or defending an idea I don't truly understand or believe in. The information I need to defend my ideas with is always there inside of me. When we combine knowledge and experience, it removes the stress from communicating our vision to others.

Whether we are in tech, business, science, philosophy, or the arts, if we're communicating a truth we have internalized, we will be open to others who question our ideas. Even if the person challenging us is antagonistic or condescending, the humility we project can remove the conflict and turn it into a constructive dialogue. It always makes me smile when the person who has challenged my ideas approaches me afterwards to apologize for "playing devil's advocate." I always tell them, "No, I welcome your argument. This discussion is valuable because it helps me evolve in my thinking." I am truly building a vision. So, when I meet people who challenge my ideas, I genuinely love it because it elevates my thinking. For me, that is priceless.

The magical thing about this layer of confidence is that it gives us the ability to turn people with negative intentions into allies. When we have the knowledge to make others understand that our vision is not about our *ego,* and that it is even beyond our *self,* we can win them over because our vision is about adding to the world.

THE ROOTS

The deepest layer of confidence is our relationship to our *self* and how we truly feel about life. Disappointment. Illness. Loss. Financial stress. Rejection. These are all part of the human experience. Without a deeply rooted inner confidence, these challenges have the potential to destroy us. But, like the roots of the tree, this confidence keeps us grounded in the world and gives us the strength to endure moments of crisis with a peaceful attitude.

Recently, a friend of mine was telling me about a personal transition he was going through. A successful businessman, he was suffering burnout and was in the process of trying to make positive changes in his life. Little by little—through meditation, reading, therapy, and spiritual retreats—he had begun to feel like he was building a stronger inner self, but something was holding him back. When I asked him how his process was going, he told me, "It's been amazing, but there's this thing that happens to me. Every morning, when I wake up, it feels like I'm choking, and I don't know how to make it stop." Gradually, he would reorient himself and feel more positive throughout the day, only for the feeling to return the next morning. I explained that what he was experiencing was anxiety.

"What do you fear?" I asked him.

Instinctively, he was resistant to the question.

"Nothing," he insisted. "I've worked on my inner self. I've made changes in my life." But, in truth, he had only been addressing those top layers of confidence.

Anxiety is a ghost that haunts us when we don't know how to define our fears. It's that crushing feeling that begins deep in the pit of our stomach. We might learn to cope with anxiety and keep it at bay, but it is always there, lurking in the hidden corners of our mind, ready to freeze our thoughts and drain our energy in moments of weakness. When we have anxiety, it's because we haven't questioned ourselves and defined our fears.

Part of building that deepest layer of confidence is having the courage to face our fears. There's nothing wrong with fear. It's a biological response that triggers our survival instincts. Fear is a much more manageable emotion than anxiety because it's a response to a specific cause. Once we define and accept the things we fear, we can start finding ways to protect ourselves.

FAILURE VS. EXPERIENCE

A key element of building true inner confidence is the way in which we relate to ourselves and to others. In life, we all find ourselves in those dramatic moments when we have come to the end of a relationship. Whether it's a toxic friendship, a romantic breakup, or a work-related dispute, what makes us unable to accept the outcome and feel destroyed by it is knowing, deep down, that we have failed because we haven't done our best or given enough to that relationship.

The way we relate to others, to our lives, and to ourselves shapes our attitude and grounds us during the most dramatic moments. The difference between failure and experience lies in our ability to be fair and just to ourselves and to others in situations that haven't evolved the way we had planned or hoped. When our relationships are based on mutual respect, and when our motivation is beyond our ego, or even our self, then we can walk away from a situation without it being a failure; it then becomes a learning experience.

CHAPTER 7

LEADING A WINNING TEAM

Building a successful team begins with our ability to inspire others to join our vision. If we surround ourselves with people who are motivated by their own agendas, our team will only be as strong as its weakest member. But, if we gather people together who live in our vision, and who are working together towards a common goal, they will empower one another to strive for greatness.

Our earliest introduction to teamwork is through family. Whether we are raised in a two-parent home with four siblings or as an only child by a single parent, being a productive member of a family requires a partnership between parent and child that is based on love and respect. The parents who fulfill their responsibility to guide and nurture will foster children with a healthy sense of belonging and self-esteem. This is done through shared responsibility and positive reinforcement.

As we get a little older, our understanding of the concept of teamwork becomes more complex. In school, we learn how to collaborate via projects where each individual is assigned a specific task. In sports, we learn that a team is constructed around players performing certain roles. The team gathers its strategic forces towards achieving a common goal: scoring. Imagine a basketball game where no one passes the ball or a soccer match where no one defends the goal. Only by working together can a team win the game.

As a child, I was fortunate to experience the power of being part of a team through my family and the bonds I shared with friends, but I wasn't always the most disciplined student. As a matter of fact, I was the type to be satisfied with average grades and to work on projects at the last minute. When it came to working in a group, sometimes I would let others do my job—and, of course, they would make sure to never include me on their team again. It was only years later, when I began building my own vision and team, that I came to understand the true meaning of teamwork and the power of collaboration.

Leading a team is a challenging responsibility. It's a lot like being a parent. Our job is to nurture, guide, and protect. My company is my life, and my team members are my extended family. I truly love each person who works with me, and I am energized by the love they give me in return. When conflict arises between them, it's like having children that don't get along. As their leader, I'm there to guide them back to harmony.

We cannot build a winning team without rules and boundaries, but we also must make sure to always cherish the team as a family. Being a leader is maintaining a positive working environment. It's directing with the right vision, and having the humility to revise our strategy when the relationship between productivity and expended energy is out of balance. Most of all, leading a winning team requires *belief*: in ourselves, in our vision, and in our team members.

DIVERSITY + AMBITION = STRENGTH

There is no perfect recipe when it comes to putting together a winning team. When we gather a group of people together around achieving a common goal, diversity in skills, ideas, and temperament brings balance and fortifies their collective purpose.

On the other hand, there is one quality that must be equal among all members: *ambition*. If there is an imbalance in the level of commitment and drive within the team, those who have the strongest desire to succeed will end up having to carry those who are satisfied with mediocrity. I always tell my team, "Don't be ashamed of what you don't know. I can teach you what you need to learn, but the one thing I cannot teach is ambition." The most basic thing I expect from everyone on my team is the desire to succeed. If you are on board, you must respect the energy of your fellow team members. Otherwise, you will end up dragging the entire group down.

PROTECT YOUR TEAM FROM THEIR OWN AMBITION

As leaders, protecting the wellbeing of our team is one of our most important responsibilities. We must look out for them better than they look out for themselves. We must be the external eye that recognizes when they are overworked and overstressed. We can have the most ambitious people on our team, but if we can't see the signs of burnout, we have failed them.

When we are working towards a vision that we believe in passionately, it fulfills us and brings positivity to our day. It can be difficult, even frightening, to detach ourselves from it, even when that's exactly what we need to do to be more productive. I always tell my team that their physical and emotional health are very important to me. If they need to take time off, but they feel they can't because they have too much work, I reassure them that with organization, they can fulfill their responsibilities to their projects *and* take the time they need to recharge their batteries. I'd rather have them go on that trip they've been dreaming of and come back stronger than to have them distracted and exhausted at the office. The key is to organize their projects before they go so they can take their phone or laptop with them and set aside a half hour or an hour a day to be connected to their work. Not only will they stay on top of their projects, they are going to enjoy the rest of their day even more because they have been productive.

Not long ago, my Chief Operating Officer got pregnant and was supposed to take time off for her maternity leave, but, as her due date approached, she kept postponing. She is so close to the company that she was reluctant to let go of her responsibilities. Week after week, she wasn't making progress on hiring an interim replacement or even mentally preparing herself for the transition in her own life. Eventually, I had to force her to deal with it and go on leave. Throughout her maternity leave, she kept working from home, and then, soon after her baby was born, she came back to work determined that this change in her life wasn't going to change *her*. She tried to resume her former rhythm, but it wasn't working for her anymore. She would be up all night caring for her newborn and then arrive at the office every morning at 8:30, exhausted and burned out. So, I sat her down and explained to her that she was in denial. Things had changed for her, and they had changed in a positive way. She had a new addition to her life, and she needed to adjust her rhythm accordingly. We came up with a plan for her to come to the office at 11:00 and to work from home two days a week. When I forced her to accept the change in her life and to create a new rhythm around it, she became much more stable and productive.

I don't want unhappy people on my team. You're not helping me or anyone else by being a martyr. You cannot be productive and make a positive contribution to the team if you feel stressed out and exhausted.

MANAGE YOUR TEAM'S ENERGY SPENDING

As a leader and a manager, I am constantly monitoring the amount of energy my team expends on a project or goal and redirecting them when they need it. I never want anyone on my team overspending time and energy on a project that is yielding little results. When there is an inequity between the amount of energy we expend and the achievement it produces, it inevitably leads to burnout.

It's easy to dismiss burnout as the result of a high-energy output, but this couldn't be further from the truth. Productivity is the best adrenalin. Nothing is more energizing than hard work that yields positive results. When we have a sense of accomplishment, it's so rewarding. Not only does it replace the energy we spend, it actually gives us more energy. Burnout comes from spending too much energy in the wrong direction without enough results.

THE CORE VALUES OF A WINNING TEAM

A couple of years ago, I had an experience with my junior staff that illustrates the importance of communication and trust between a leader and her team. At the time, we had a lot of management that was older, so I had been recruiting people in their twenties who could bring a youthful energy to our mission and grow with my company. After a few months, I began to notice that they were in a place where everyone was getting along and working well together, but the results were not there and productivity was very low.

When there is a breakdown in my team, I always look to myself first. As their leader, it is my responsibility to identify the underlying issues and offer solutions. I called an emergency meeting and shared with them my disappointment and frustration. But, I also recognized that it was my responsibility to clearly define my expectations to them. I started talking to them and asking them questions about the relationship between a team, a company, and its leader.

From that dialogue, we defined a set of core values that clarified my expectations of them:

- *Respect and commitment* to the team and its overall growth, as opposed to focusing on the success of our own tasks, creates an emotional link between the individual and the team and builds a trust that is essential to success. Each team member has responsibilities to the others, and those responsibilities are equal, if not similar.

- *Productivity* is measured in the quality of time and energy spent to accomplish a mission. When we accomplish daily tasks, it energizes the team and takes us one step closer to achieving our collective goals.

- *Regularity* comes with balance and discipline. When we have highs and lows, we lose in productivity because we are not being consistent in our work. The team member who overcomes their ups and downs and understands that hard work is an everyday mission will start experiencing tremendous growth and success within their mission and within the company.

- *Engagement* outside of work means we don't just switch off at the end of the day. I expect my team to bring me inspiration from their life experience. My mission does not stop when I leave the office. Whenever and wherever I am in the world, I am always working for my company and my team.

Once we had defined these four values and they understood what was expected of them on a daily basis as individuals and as collaborative members of a team, productivity soared. By including their voice in the conversation, and allowing them to contribute to defining what it means to be part of a team, we established a mutual trust. To this day, many of them are still with Mayshad, and I have been so proud to watch them grow in both their salaries and their responsibilities.

These values are applicable to any winning team in any industry anywhere in the world. They are fundamental to our professional projects, as well as to our personal ones. When we give that level of commitment to all aspects of our lives, we can achieve amazing results. It is through joining our path to others who share our vision and commitment to life that the true power of teamwork begins.

CHAPTER 8

TO BE OR NOT TO BE SINGLE

In an era when Internet relationships, gender fluidity, and single parenting are on the rise, the traditional structure of a committed relationship has been completely redefined. Gender-specific roles that were the norm just a generation ago no longer apply. In today's world, a wife is free to pursue a career while her husband chooses to stay home with the kids. In fact, we no longer feel the same pressure to commit to another person in order to find the kind of stability that just half a century ago could only be found within the construct of a conventional marriage.

The days of the stereotypical stay-at-home wife and breadwinner husband are over. Marriage is no longer something you need in order to be successful or financially secure. More and more, people are shifting away from the pursuit of happily-ever-after, and focusing their energy on their professional lives. By the time we reach our twenties, most of us will have experienced how difficult and heartbreaking a failed relationship can be. Investing time and energy in our careers brings stability to our lives, whereas a fragile new relationship is so often fraught with uncertainty.

On the other hand, if the thousands of dating and relationship apps on the market are any indication, we also seem unable to totally give up on the concept of commitment. As human beings, we have a primal need for love and companionship. For many of us, career success becomes hollow if, ultimately, we do not find someone with whom we can share our lives. So, where does that leave us? Caught somewhere between striving for fulfillment in our professional and personal lives, yet unable to truly find it in either realm.

But, what if it's not a question of either/or? What if we can apply the same leadership principals that make us successful in our professional lives to building a successful relationship? By approaching our relationship as our "Life Project," it gives us the clarity to accept the shift away from a traditional couple who are no longer relevant in today's world, and create a new structure that is adapted to the needs of the modern couple. It is a structure where we:

- No longer need to be in a relationship to feel socially successful.
- No longer need to live under the same roof to raise happy children.
- No longer need to be bound by antiquated gender roles.

In the modern couple, we build an equal and supportive partnership by communicating with each other in order to create a relationship structure that has the capacity to adapt and evolve under pressure from external forces. A healthy and fulfilling relationship is possible when we share the same vision, evolve in a common direction, and support each other in the success of our mutual accomplishments.

KNOW YOUR SELF

Just as our path to leadership begins with a journey of introspection that leads to a greater understanding of self, the first step to building a successful relationship is knowing and accepting who *you* are, and knowing what you want and don't want in a partner.

A big mistake people often make going into a new relationship is either trying to adapt who they are, or, worse, subconsciously expecting the other person to adapt to them. Over time, this inevitably leads to frustration and disappointment. When a relationship is shiny and new, it's easy to be blinded by the power of attraction, but imagine how much time and heartache we could save if we were simply honest with ourselves and our partner about who we are and what we want.

Applying leadership to our personal lives means being in a relationship where we are true to ourselves and our partner accepts who we are. Once we have created this foundation of mutual respect and understanding, then we can work on improving ourselves within the relationship.

SHARE A LIFE MISSION

The most iconic modern couples, from Barrack and Michele to Jay-Z and Beyoncé, have endured personal and professional struggles and have emerged stronger because they are, first and foremost, a partnership built around a shared vision of life.

Just as we create a vision or mission statement in our professional lives, defining who we are together and what we want to achieve as a couple creates a unifying clarity of purpose. Having a coherent vision related to the identity of our union brings passion into our shared journey and allows us to evolve as individuals within a relationship.

ENVISION A PLAN FOR THE FUTURE

Every relationship begins with a spark of passion that leads to the desire to take on the challenge of merging two lives into a single, shared path. Clearly defining the direction of that path removes the doubts that may unconsciously undermine the relationship.

Sit with your partner and do the exercise of projecting yourselves five years into the future. Outline a detailed vision, with shared goals and expectations. Discussing the future as a couple can be scary. But, ultimately, it will make us feel more secure within the relationship and prepare us to overcome the challenges we face in life together.

WORK TOGETHER AS A TEAM

In our professional lives, we build a successful team by assessing the strengths of each individual member and assigning tasks accordingly. This not only boosts productivity, it creates harmony within the team because individual roles are clearly defined and everyone knows what is expected of them.

If we look at the modern couple like a team, then we can apply those same principals to building a healthy relationship based on mutual respect. Defining our roles validates who we are as individuals within the relationship and gives us a shared responsibility for the life we are building together.

COMPROMISE IS A TWO-WAY STREET

Just as we did with building our healthy ecosystem, a strong relationship requires that we establish rules and communicate them to one another. Those rules need to apply to *us*, as well. We don't ask for what we can't give ourselves.

We all come into a relationship with what I like to think of as a little bottle of compromise. If our partner is making compromise after compromise to be with us, at some point, that bottle will run dry and they are going to lose patience with us and the relationship. In the modern couple, there is a natural balance between give and take that empowers both individuals and strengthens the bonds of the relationship.

DANCE TO THE SAME RHYTHM

Selecting a partner who is equally as ambitious and driven in life as we are is a critical component of the modern couple. It's not about being similar and having the same background. It's about sharing the same lifestyle and rhythm. Differences in culture, religion, and career choices can be complementary because diversity enriches the structure of the relationship. Opposites can and do attract, but what makes it work is when the two people have rhythms and visions that are in sync.

On any given week, I might be in Paris on Monday, Los Angeles on Wednesday, and Marrakesh for the weekend before flying to New York for a conference the following week. Imagine if I had someone waiting for me at home who did not share my rhythm. My passion for travel and commitment to my work would naturally lead to frustration and resentment, and the relationship wouldn't last long.

Think of it like two people on a winding country road. If one wants to run, but the other prefers to walk, there is no harmony of purpose. Either one drags the other one down, or one is held back. On the other hand, if *both* choose to walk, they will enjoy their leisurely pace as they talk and take in the scenery together. By that same token, the couple who chooses to run down that country road *together* will share in the thrill of the wind in their faces and the exhilaration of adrenalin.

FREE YOURSELF FROM JUDGMENT

When a relationship isn't empowering or fulfilling, it's easy to assign blame to the other person. It absolves us of our own accountability, and, on some level, it just feels good to be angry. But, we can lose ourselves in judgment and become prisoners of our own anger.

A leader is always accountable for his or her actions; non-leaders start pointing fingers when a relationship fails. I know so many people who go through a divorce or breakup and say, "It's not my fault." But, the truth is, there are two people in a relationship, and each is equally accountable to the other. I take full responsibility for everything that happens in my life. When my marriage ended, I knew the reason was because I had evolved, and I had to be fair to my former husband. I wanted to become a leader in the United Nations, and it didn't fit with the lifestyle I had back then. I was not going to drag him along on my journey when what he truly wanted was a quiet, calm life with a wife at home. I told him, "We're not separating. Our relationship is simply evolving into something else that is fair to both of us."

When we judge others, we waste energy that we should be spending on our own growth and evolution. If we feel the person we are in a relationship with is dragging us down or draining our energy, it's our responsibly to ourselves and to the relationship to make the healthy life choice to either accept our partner for who they are or have the courage to walk away. Even after a relationship ends, we are often consumed by bitterness and resentment, but when that happens, we are still trapped in the dysfunction of the relationship; we just don't realize it.

Only by letting go of the emotional baggage of a negative relationship can we start turning anger and frustration into compassion. Compassion is true freedom. It breaks the chains that bind us to a person who is bringing negativity into our lives, and it truly frees us to begin striving for a partnership that empowers us.

REGULARLY SET NEW GOALS

Human beings are designed for movement. But, as we have evolved, our lives have become increasingly static. In just a few centuries, we have gone from warriors and hunter-gatherers to living in cities and suburbs, surrounded by creature comforts that isolate us from our survival instincts. When we don't have that movement in our lives and we don't have goals we can share with our partner in order to be productive together, we start channeling our subconscious frustrations and pent-up energy into battling each other.

When we take on a project or task at work, we are constantly analyzing our achievements, readjusting our direction, and setting new goals. In the Life Project of our relationship, we must take a similar approach if we are to advance together as a team. Getting married, buying a home, and having children are all common goals that we set for ourselves at the outset of a new relationship, but for the modern couple to survive and flourish, we need to regularly set new goals in order to reaffirm our commitment to one another.

The union of two souls is no longer driven by survival or procreation. It's a choice we make daily to continue walking the same path as our partner. By regularly analyzing our shared vision and setting new goals, we empower one another to evolve within the relationship.

CHAPTER 9

THE HEALTHY LIFESTYLE

Life is a playful journey. Its natural ups and downs should inspire us to create a balance between the different aspects of our lives in order to construct a harmonious inner self.

Healthy living is more than just working out or eating our veggies. It's a lifestyle that leads to clarity of body, mind, and soul.

The world is full of talented and creative people with boundless potential who fall into a toxic lifestyle. They are so driven by negative impulses that, while they may be gifted, they will never become leaders. A true leader is able to maintain clarity regardless of whether they are rewarded with success or confronted by failure. What gives us the strength to maintain balance through the highs and lows of life is a healthy, disciplined routine. It doesn't have to be an obsession. A healthy lifestyle should become such a positive ritual that it's as easy and intuitive to perform as breathing.

On our path of leadership, our energy is our biggest asset. It's the fuel that keeps us moving forward in the pursuit of our dreams. When we have been working towards a long-term goal and we achieve it, we experience a rush of adrenalin that fills us with joyful energy. But, there are also micro goals within our reach that we can achieve on a daily basis that produce a similar boost to our energy levels. I like to begin my day with the goal of working out for one hour. When I achieve that goal, it makes me feel powerful because I've already begun my day with a sense of accomplishment. As a result, my mind and body think: *If I can achieve* this, *I can achieve other things in my day.*

Accessing leadership in our healthy lifestyle is the process of harnessing the powerful energy produced by feeding our three bodies: the physical, the intellectual, and the spiritual. A healthy lifestyle is the core of success. In order to lead others, we have to be driven by our higher motivations. We can't be ruled by external forces (or even internal ones that are tied to our egos). The one who is healthy in body, mind, and soul will elevate his or herself to a state of leadership that is driven by clarity of vision and purpose.

DON'T WAIT FOR THE NEW YEAR TO MAKE A RESOLUTION

The natural question for someone who is not instinctively drawn to a healthy lifestyle is, "How do I start?" When deciding to make healthy lifestyle changes, the biggest mistake people make right out of the gate is setting a deadline: "On January 1, I'm changing my life." That seldom works. More often than not, what really ends up happening is that we change for a day or a month before returning to our old habits.

If you're ready to make a change, make it now. It doesn't matter if it's in the middle of the year, the middle of the week, or the middle of the day. Just do it. By postponing the start date, we invariably give ourselves an excuse to indulge in a habit or behavior we've already acknowledged as negative—or, at least, not productive. If it's Friday and we decide to start a diet on Monday, what ends up happening? In anticipation of the change, we eat more than we would have in the first place and wind up starting that diet on Monday carrying additional weight.

Don't give yourself deadlines to implement healthy changes in your life. It needs to start the moment you're ready. And, it doesn't start with drastic changes. It starts with one positive thing at a time. The healthy lifestyle is all about striving for consistency and balance. If we want to start running, we don't have to begin by training for a marathon. We can start by running around the block. Any positive step in the right direction is a productive step in setting us on a path to change.

TRADE GUILT FOR BALANCE

I am attracted to positivity, and I'm now instinctively drawn to things that will empower my day and give me energy that I can channel into being productive—but that wasn't always the case for me. When I went off to college and found myself with the freedom to make my own choices about my lifestyle, I made some pretty classic mistakes.

I had a textbook case of the "Freshman 15." I'd binge on junk food and starches and then feel guilty about it. Halfway through the semester, I realized my jeans were a little tighter than they should be, so I decided I needed to lose two pounds—and, in trying to lose those two pounds, I ended up gaining twenty. I would start my day saying, "I'm going to make up for yesterday by not eating anything today." Of course (after avoiding breakfast and denying myself a healthy midmorning snack), by lunchtime, I was thinking like a starving person. I'd be sitting at a table with my friends and my resolve would completely crumble. I'd fill myself up with breads or pastas (carbs that would satisfy my hunger, but which I wasn't burning off with exercise). Then I would feel guilty about it because I didn't make the right choices. By the afternoon, I would think to myself, "Well, I've already ruined my diet for today. I might as well binge the rest of the day."

The next morning, I'd get on my scale and be greeted by an extra pound. Now, I didn't just have two pounds to lose, I had three. So, with the same self-defeating logic, I would vow to starve myself for the day all over again—with the same results. It became a vicious cycle. When I went back home for break at the end of that first semester, of course everyone in my family kept remarking on how much weight I had gained. (*Like I didn't already know. I'd only been weighing myself daily and struggling with my diet for the last three months. But, thanks for pointing it out.*) This put even more pressure on me. As my clothes got tighter and tighter, I refused to buy anything in a bigger size and started wearing all black to cover myself up and not stand out.

This went on for about a year, and then something amazing happened. I met someone who didn't know me before I had gained the weight, and they liked me the way I was—all extra twenty pounds of me. So, I decided to accept myself: *This is the new me and I'm happy with it.* I stopped torturing myself with guilt and trying to deprive myself of the food that I needed to fuel my body throughout the day. I ate when I was hungry, and I enjoyed my food. I bought some new clothes (in the right size) and starting feeling good about myself. Because I had more energy, little by little, I started working out more. You can guess what happened, right? You got it. I started losing the weight naturally because I was no longer on that rollercoaster ride of binge and guilt.

When we start eating because we enjoy it, we naturally gravitate towards foods that are healthier for us. A healthy lifestyle doesn't mean kale and carrot sticks for breakfast, lunch, and dinner. It's a balanced approach that begins with introducing healthy choices. Feeling guilty about breaches to our healthy lifestyle only breeds frustration. It does not help us find solutions. At the core of guilt is the failure to accept the truth of a situation. Acceptance is an act of maturity and accountability. Searching for the origin of our mistake is the best step to recovering from it.

Now that I travel almost every week for work, the temptation to skip a workout or cheat on my diet with a cheese plate somewhere over the Atlantic is something I'm faced with regularly. Thankfully, I do not always breach my healthy lifestyle. But, if I do succumb to temptation or have a moment of weakness (because perfection is a daily quest that we do not always achieve), I catch up by balancing the next day with healthier choices.

Not only is guilt unproductive, it can have unexpected consequences. When we feel bad about the food we're eating, it stresses our digestion. When I don't torment myself after indulging in a big meal, I digest it well and wake up the next morning feeling less hungry. As a result, I will eat less over the course of the day. I'm able to trick myself with balance.

HEALTHY BODY

Every time I go on a trip with my mother, as soon as we get on the plane, she'll turn to me and say, "I'm on a diet. I'm only going to have one soup a day." She's absolutely convinced of it. But, not only does my mother not starve herself for the week, she ends up tormenting herself the entire time when she should be relaxing and enjoying her vacation. Depriving ourselves never works. It only perpetuates the cycle of indulgence and guilt.

Be realistic about your diet. Understand your eating habits and metabolism and try to make healthier choices. If I have a week of not eating healthy, I will observe myself and ask *why*. I will dig until I find the source. Am I suffering emotional stress? Is it my hormones? Is it a lack of sleep? When I find the source, it will lead me to the solution.

Observe your body. Learn to recognize the signs that a craving has become a habit. I love chocolate. It's my weakness. If I have a craving for it in the late afternoon, I'm not going to feel guilty about it. But, if the next day, at the same time, I have another call for chocolate, I will question myself. It's not a coincidence. It's because my cravings are training my body to tell me at 4:00 in the afternoon that I need chocolate. So, I will resist the craving and break that habit for a couple of days and then eat chocolate when *I* want to eat it, instead of when my body tells me.

Understand your body. Respect it. Be playful with it. When your body orders you to do things that result in a bad routine or habit, you need to tell it, "Hey, *I'm* the one in control here." Then distract yourself with positive activities. Throw yourself back into work or go for a run with your powerful playlist. Turn it into a challenge. Play with your food. Make meals that look beautiful. Surround yourself with colorful, glistening foods, like nuts, berries, and yogurts. Make them a part of your diet because they look beautiful, taste delicious, and they're full of vitamins.

Don't fight hunger. Eat if you're hungry. The biggest trick is not to wait to feel hungry again to eat something because we'll be more likely to overdo it. Eat a small, healthy snack every two hours. I always have almonds and sundried fruits in my bag. Sometimes, I'll even eat a handful with a glass of water before heading to a restaurant so I don't jump headfirst into a three-course meal. If I'm not starving, I'll order with my mind and not with my stomach.

When I arrive at a stage of actual hunger, it takes me into a process. My mind sends a signal that says: *Eat!* I am an achiever, so when I arrive at dinner and my mind orders me to eat, I am going to eat the whole table. Eventually, I realize I should never have let myself get to that stage. The minute I start feeling a little signal that tells me, "Hmm, I could have something to eat," I know I need to grab a healthy snack from my bag to stop that message from turning into a command. As fierce as I am in my positive activities, I can channel the same energy into my negative impulses, as well. This is my personality. Every positive thing has a downside to it, so my strong, dynamic attitude can be in everything, even eating.

A healthy body is not about being thin or obsessively working out. It's about a balanced diet and an active lifestyle. Exercise doesn't just happen in the gym. Exercise is walking to the supermarket, riding a bike to work, or going for a hike or long walk on the weekend. Be active in whatever way you can as regularly as you can.

HEALTHY MIND

Creating a healthy lifestyle for our intellectual body is about discovering and being receptive to knowledge that stimulates our intellect. It's in the music we listen to, the books we read, and even the media we expose ourselves to. It's all those things that keep our minds growing and give us inspiration and ideas we can apply to our life mission and professional projects. It's eye-opening activities that are not directly related to our industry, but that will automatically bring richness to what we do.

Make things that nourish your intellect a part of your daily routine. Instead of surfing the Internet an hour before bed, read a few chapters of a book with empowering content. Take a Sunday afternoon and go to a gallery or museum to expose yourself to art and culture. Just as we avoid putting junk food into our physical bodies, we need to be constantly mindful of the quality of the content we are putting into our minds.

Leading a healthy intellectual lifestyle is aiming for quality over quantity. It's how we consume things—from the way we shop to the way we absorb information and entertainment. It's understanding on a deeper level the choices we make and the consequences and impact of those choices. We don't just go to a theater every Saturday and watch whatever happens to be on the screen. We research what's out there and read reviews. Having a process in place for everything our minds consume is how we put a premium on quality. Empowerment starts with the direction we give to our choices.

Cultivating an interest in other people's talent and ideas helps us grow as leaders. The mind is a muscle. The more active it is, the stronger it becomes. Whether we have graduated from college with a degree in Finance or in Fashion, when we combine that knowledge with a passion for something outside our field of expertise, our minds open like flowers to the light of the world and we begin to draw inspiration from the most unexpected sources.

HEALTHY SOUL

Being healthy in our spiritual bodies is giving ourselves a refuge from the noise that surrounds us at all times. It's taking a break from the pressures of society and the demands of our daily lives. It's the distance we give ourselves from our lives and our projects in order to come back with renewed energy and a clear mind.

It's in our moments of meditation. It's in our connection with nature. It's in our time alone when we disconnect from external influences. Sometimes I'm on my phone so much it becomes a source of stress in my life. When that happens, I force myself to take a night off. Technology is wonderful until we find it is taking over our lives. Taking time to unplug allows us to refocus on our families, our relationships, or even just on feeding our own minds.

We need to be *in* control of things, not controlled *by* them. Even the most positive impulses can become negative if we allow them to rule our lives. An impulse becomes negative when we are unable to manage it. When our cravings become regular, it becomes an addiction. If we become stressed over not being able to do something (whether it's eating, working out, or being on our phone) that's a sure sign we have crossed the line between pleasure and addiction. Addiction doesn't just apply with drugs and alcohol; it's anything we do to the extreme. The moment we allow something to rule us, it becomes an addiction. If we become dependent on something, then we are no longer in balance. Pure balance is constant work. It's not being a slave to anything, but choosing everything every day.

TRUE FREEDOM

A line that's easy to cross is the one between being free and being lost. In college, I decided to study hotel and restaurant management, mainly because the program allowed me the opportunity to travel every six months. I had more passion for the travel than I did for the program, which became evident when I got fired from an internship with a luxury hotel in Milan because I was so immersed in the city's night life that I got caught by my manager sleeping on the job—literally.

Many of the guests at the hotel were football players for A.C. Milan, which was fun when we got to interact with them, but the management was strict, the staff was old, and setting up banquet rooms for hotel events wasn't exactly the most stimulating activity for a twenty-two-year-old with a fierce appetite for adventure. I was in the program with a friend, and one of the bartenders noticed how bored we were. He told us he had a friend who owned a restaurant and said he could get us waitressing jobs if we wanted to earn a little extra money on the side.

We started working at the restaurant at night, and then working at the hotel all day. We were having the time of our lives, meeting new people and partying all night. The next morning, we would show up to our internship exhausted, so my friend and I would take turns napping in a chair in the corner of one of the banquet rooms. Then, one day the manager of the hotel called to inform us that they were letting us go—which also meant we were out on the street. We thought we were being slick, but we were so obvious that it didn't take long for them to catch on that it was taking us three hours to set up one banquet table. Of course, we were scared to tell our parents we'd been fired, and we were having so much fun working at this cool restaurant in Milan that we certainly didn't want to go home.

To preempt them notifying our parents, we called the director of the program at our college and told him our parents were so unhappy with the internship we had been doing, they had found us another internship at a different hotel. Then, through a contact at the restaurant, we found ourselves a new apartment, and with our jobs at the restaurant we could afford the rent. We solved the situation in two hours. Now we were free—or so I thought.

After that, we went out partying until 3:00 every morning and slept all day. When we woke up the next day, it would already be dark out, so I was living this truly nocturnal life-style. It was fun at first, having that freedom to do whatever I wanted whenever I wanted. But, after a few weeks, I started to feel weird about it. Then, one day I questioned myself, "Am I experiencing freedom, or am I getting lost in this life-style?" That's when I began to understand what the concept of true freedom is.

We all have a perimeter in which we can navigate freely, but if we don't take the time to look around and see where the healthy borders are, we can easily wander into a direc-tionless existence. I had crossed over that line. At some point, I realized that the life I was living, though fun and adventur-ous, was not leading me anywhere productive.

True freedom is having the humility to question our-selves in order to maintain direction in our lives. We are lost when we have no structure or purpose. Of course, we have the right to change course and explore, but as we reorient, we must always be mindful that we are living a lifestyle with purpose and conviction.

CHAPTER 10

CHOOSE YOUR BATTLES

No matter how organized we are in our life plan, no matter how healthy our lifestyle, and no matter how much work we've done on empowering our inner self, the fact remains that there are only twenty-four hours in a day. From China to Chattanooga, from seven to seventy-seven years old, from the billionaire CEO to the peddler in the local market, this is the common thread that links every single soul on this beautiful planet.

The most valuable measure in the world is time, and our biggest asset is our energy. Never waste time and energy fighting a losing battle or supporting the wrong cause. A leader goes into a battle for a greater purpose, not just to make a point or for the pleasure of the fight. There is a cause behind it, and there is a solution. In a battle, there is always a huge expenditure of energy. A leader must have principals, and an exit strategy if the negative toll becomes too high.

WHEN THEY GO LOW, YOU GO HIGH

Whenever I am drawn into a conflict, I always remind myself of something my grandfather used to say when I was a little girl: "If a dog bites you, are you going to get down on your knees and bite him back?" In other words: Never lower yourself to someone else's level.

Our actions define who we are. A true leader never allows an opponent to pull them into a strategy or behavior that is beneath them. Do you want to be the kind of person who relies on their intellect and influence, or the kind who uses underhanded tactics and low blows? Not only is distancing ourselves from toxic people the best defense, it's also the most efficient way to fight back. Keeping a cool head and a noble attitude towards people who are being aggressive and impulsive puts us on the high road, and will, ultimately, give us the advantage.

IMPULSIVITY IS THE ENEMY

When someone puts me in a situation where I need to fight back, I always take at least twenty-four hours to decide how to respond. Never react to a conflict right away. Responding impulsively more often than not leads to errors in both judgment and strategy. Take the time to calmly devise your strategy before acting on it. When we are caught off guard and respond to a conflict immediately, we tend to react with our emotions and not with our minds.

Reaction is ego-driven. It's that knee-jerk impulse to hit back. This does nothing but scratch the itch to fight. In reality, the problem we think we're solving is going to come back because we didn't really find the source of it. Instead of pointing the finger at others, always question yourself when there is struggle or challenge. This is something I tell my team. When we experience a setback, I will tell them, "I do not blame anyone but us." In any conflict, at the very least, we are responsible for putting ourselves in that difficult situation in the first place. The energy we expend looking for some external force to blame is energy we could be directing towards solving the problem.

When we are led by our impulses, what often happens is, the next day, the next week, maybe even a year later, we look back at ourselves in that moment and it seems almost like a completely different person from who we really are. We may have thought there was no other option at the time, but with distance, we now see the solution (because there is always a solution to a real problem), and we realize how wrong we were. Accidents happen, but the most important thing is to analyze our behavior afterwards and learn from our mistake how counterproductive it was to react impulsively.

We will never become the leaders we aim to be if we lose control of our emotions. We face challenges, large and small, every single day; how we *choose* to react to them is entirely up to us. Even the most powerful CEO is put to the test when she gets into her car and, after sitting in traffic for forty frustrating minutes, is cut off by an aggressive driver. The one who loses her temper and allows the encounter to put her into a negative state gives up all her power. She carries that negativity with her throughout her day and allows it to drain her most valuable resource: her energy.

If someone who is not half as successful as we are can take us out of positive thinking and put us in a negative state, then that person has gained power over us. When we can't back down from a fight we don't belong in, it's our ego keeping us there. When we react impulsively without taking time to consider the consequences of our actions, our ego is clouding our judgment. The ego fools us into not finding the real cause of a problem. We must trust only in our inner self to lead us to a solution. True power is mastery of our impulses and emotions in moments of conflict or stress.

LET GO OF LITTLE IRRITATIONS

With a healthy lifestyle, throughout the day we are filling ourselves with energy through positive practices, which we then channel into creative thinking and productivity. It's a constant balancing act between the energy we bring in and the energy we expend. If we are caught up in focusing on all the small irritations in our day, then, when we're faced with real challenges and struggles, we won't have the energy or clarity to solve them. When our minds are full of noise, we lose the ability to appreciate the positivity in our lives, and we don't have the energy to solve the things that matter. Choosing our battles is channeling our energy and strength into the right direction.

We all go through phases in our lives where we are confronted with struggles that are beyond our control. Whether it's financial stress, a breakup, or an illness, we are in a situation that is extracting a huge amount of energy from us. We need to replace that energy by being even more vigilant about caring for our physical, mental, and spiritual health. We're no good to ourselves, or anyone around us, if we are run down from lack of sleep or poor nutrition, or if we are disconnected from our spirituality. When we are faced with true challenges, it's the healthy lifestyle we fall back on to provide the energy to persevere.

Some people will ignore big struggles. They stick their heads in the sand and say, "No, no. It's fine. I'm strong." Not only are they not looking for a solution, they're allowing the problem to fester and worsen. Recognizing and respecting a real struggle when we face it is one of the main criterions of leadership. I know people who do just the reverse. They are totally caught up in the minutia of their day, ignoring real problems until they become completely unmanageable. A true leader has the clarity to see beyond the small things, and the discipline to conserve energy for tackling the bigger issues.

KNOW WHEN THE BATTLE IS OVER

When I am fighting for something I believe in, I am fierce in battle, but the moment I achieve my goal, I move on. One big mistake I see people making routinely, especially in the humanitarian world, is getting hung up on the fight and not knowing when to walk away. When we get hooked on the adrenalin that comes from the fight, we lose sight of our vision and the wellbeing of the people who support us.

Winning a battle is not always about getting the outcome we wanted. It's about staying strong in the face of struggle and surviving to fight another day. Clinging to an objective or outcome that is becoming increasingly unattainable will tempt us into a strategy that is beneath us. Leaders must always take care to watch out that they don't compromise their values, and that the battle doesn't impact the greatness of their cause. If we lose ourselves in the fight, we are at risk of putting the community that is supporting us in danger.

As leaders, we are never alone in facing our struggles. We have people who believe in us and trust in our vision, so we need to be able to walk away from a situation that can become toxic for them—even when the result is not exactly what we would have wanted it to be. A leader is not supposed to be invincible. Not only are we responsible for managing our own energy, we must always care for the wellbeing of our team, our friends, and our family. Never drag them through a conflict that has become toxic. A leader understands that life is about building a vision. The real fight is for a greater self and a greater world.

CHAPTER 11

COMMUNICATE FOR GREATER IMPACT

"Communication" is one of those buzz words that we hear a lot in both our personal and professional lives. We hear advice like, "Communication is the core of a healthy relationship,"

or "Communication is the key to success," but what do those phrases really mean? It seems that the more communication becomes an integral part of our daily lives, the broader and vaguer a concept it becomes. In terms of strong leadership, communication is the ability to convey a message to others in a way that makes it both appealing and meaningful to them. It's inspiring others to follow your vision and achieve their own greatness.

How successful we are as communicators depends on two things: first, how well we understand our own message; and, second, our ability to speak the same language as our audience. When we are in the process of shaping a message, the first thing we must always do is identify *who* our audience is. The language I use when I speak to a group of scientists at a conference is not the same language I use when I speak to students in a classroom. A skilled communicator has the ability to adapt to his or her audience so their message can be understood by anyone, regardless of age, education, or industry.

There are so many subtle nuances in how we transmit and receive information, and they are related to our perceptions and past experiences. We all have our own path and our own anxieties and fears that make us react dramatically to certain situations. A skilled communicator has the ability to be sensitive to others and compassionate about their struggles. Only then can we truly understand our audience and what language they speak. It's like tuning a radio to the right frequency that clears the static and transmits our message loud and clear.

The language we use to communicate our ideas or vision should be simple and clear enough for the people in front of us to understand it. We're not impressing anyone with our knowledge by using big words; we're just making it more difficult for them to understand us. The type of person who is so intellectually superior that they can only communicate their ideas to people on the same level of education or sophistication is limiting the scope and impact of their message. When we learn to communicate in a way that is accessible to everyone, we stop being self-centered in the way we transmit our convictions and open our vision to the world.

ONE-TO-ONE COMMUNICATION

Once we have done the hard work of defining who we are, what we want out of life, and what we need to do to get there, the next step is conveying this message to the people in our personal lives: our friends, our family, and our significant others. Unfortunately, it's often those closest to us with whom we have the most difficulty communicating.

Our families have been with us all of our lives, so it can be difficult for them to see us as independent grownups. Subconsciously, they will always see us as fragile children, and, subconsciously, that's the role we often revert to when we're around them. Our families want us to be happy. They want success for us, and they want to support our choices, but they can also feed our doubts and insecurities if we're not careful in the way we communicate ourselves to them. My relationship with my own family changed for the better when I finally learned to embrace the person I wanted to become. I wasn't always able to communicate my vision to them clearly, but I knew what I was going to build was steeped in the values that would make them proud of me. Once I learned how to communicate with confidence what I was trying to achieve, they were able to let go and trust in my path.

There is our conscious self, the person we have chosen to become, and then there is the subconscious part of our mind that is linked to our past. Family triggers the dormant child in all of us, and that influences our behavior around them without us even being aware of it. We need to be able to detach ourselves from this influence by finding the right emotional distance from our families. We're better off sharing our doubts with an expert in our field, or even with a stranger in the street, who will be more objective than our families. When we do discuss our life choices or vision with our families, we must project confidence and strength. Once we are able to do this, it smoothes out the rough edges around our relationship with our families.

Our friends don't trigger our past, but they can sometimes subconsciously keep us tethered to our present. A friend who does not share our dynamic need to move forward with positive ambition will always be scared to lose us, so they succumb to petty emotions like jealousy, judgment, and guilt. Friendships should bring as much positive energy into our lives as we put back into them. No family ties or marriage contracts obligate us to maintain a relationship that does not bring positivity in our lives. If we feel drained by a friendship, we let go of it. As leaders, our role is to empower and inspire others. We share our knowledge and achievements in order to improve, not just our own lives, but the lives of others, as well. We can't afford to have toxic people around us who keep a running tally of canceled brunches and delayed birthday wishes.

When two people meet and fall in love, their communication is focused around sharing with one another who they are. As time goes on and infatuation fades, we often stop connecting with one another on this intimate level, and that's when the relationship begins to struggle. We may have the home, the children, and all of the trappings of a successful couple, but there is no harmony of purpose. Irritations become issues, which in turn become divisions, and, before we know it, two people who once loved each other are consumed by resentment and anger. We are constantly evolving as human beings; what we want and what we don't want changes as we grow. What truly holds two people together is their capacity to create and sustain a mutual vision for their lives.

Being clear in the way we project ourselves to the people in our lives strengthens the bonds we share with those closest to us. The better we know ourselves and the better we are able to express the fundamentals of our lives (what gives us positivity, what drives us, and what drains our energy), the healthier our relationships become.

PROFESSIONAL COMMUNICATION

I used to be shy around communicating to the media all the great work we do through the Mayshad Foundation. I wanted our accomplishments to speak for themselves. Then I read something that completely changed my perception: "Doing business without advertising is like winking at a girl in the dark." You know what you're doing, but no one else does.

Sharing the story of our hard work and the accomplishments we've had throughout our professional careers makes our work more impactful. The success of our communication on a professional level is in our coherence. We have to share what we do, but we also have to do what we're sharing. If the story we're telling is not completely true, it's not sustainable over time.

Great leaders and communicators are always in control of their messages. Rather than let someone else control how our story unfolds, we control how that information is presented.

At Mayshad, we create good content in-house that we provide to the media. We make their job easier, and, at the same time, we ensure the quality of the message is in keeping with our vision. Life is all about perception and communication, and that is both a skill and an art. If you can communicate well, you can do anything.

GLOBAL COMMUNICATION

Some people use social media to build a network of friends. Some people use it to keep up with family. Some use it for ecommerce. Perhaps its most relevant and impactful role in our lives today is as a powerful tool of influence. Social media is where you share your story with the world: the story of your business, the story of your own inner development, and the story behind your vision.

I've never been on social media to make new friends or keep in touch with old classmates. I came late to platforms like Facebook and Instagram because I thought attracting attention to who I am and what I do was a waste of time. Once I began to shape my vision and had a message to pass on, I realized what an amazing outlet it was and began using it as a vehicle to amplify my voice and inspire others.

Recently, a young woman reached out to me for advice about starting a blog. I told her that successful content is all about storytelling. It's having quality images and a story behind each post. We have to look at our social media with an editorial eye, as if we are editors of a magazine or curators of an art exhibition. Successful storytelling makes people sensitive to our lives, to our struggles, and to our achievements. Our content should put people on our life journey.

CHAPTER 12

SUCCESSFUL ENTREPRENEURSHIP 101

Entrepreneurship begins with finding a passion or a talent we can develop into a business. How successful that business becomes depends on the strength of our strategy and the amount of time and productivity we devote to building something from the ground up.

Recently, I was having lunch with a former employee who left Mayshad to start her own entrepreneurial venture. She had been on her own for about six months and the first thing she said to me when I asked her how she was doing was, "Oh, my God, it's never ending. I'm working 24/7 now."

That is what entrepreneurship is.

It's more than a job; it's a way of life.

Employees have structured working hours and can disconnect at the end of the day. Freelancers must be disciplined in order to manage their time and productivity. An entrepreneur is responsible not only for the success of his or her business, but also for the wellbeing of all the people who depend on the strength of his or her vision and ambition. For the entrepreneur, there is no such thing as nine to five. We are constantly developing our connections, searching for new clients and investors, sourcing materials, figuring out ways to scale our business, and dreaming up bigger and better ways to achieve our goals.

I work sixteen hours a day, seven days a week, 365 days a year. My drive to succeed does not switch off when I leave the office at the end of the day. From the moment I wake up in the morning to the moment I lay my head down to sleep at night, wherever I am in the world, I am working for Mayshad. The beauty of combining strong leadership with a powerful vision is that you can engage and inspire a team that feels the same level of commitment. At Mayshad, *my* sixteen hours is multiplied by each member of my team's sixteen hours. Thus, our productivity becomes exponentially more powerful.

Time that could be spent just having a social life is time an entrepreneur devotes to networking and attending industry conferences to build professional connections. Time that could be spent reading books or watching movies for pure entertainment is time an entrepreneur focuses on acquiring knowledge and advice from other professionals with experiences and expertise in our field. We're constantly feeding ourselves with information that will help us develop our entrepreneurial skills and become leaders in our industry.

SEEK OUT THREE MENTORS

One of my favorite things about the level of success I have achieved is that I now have the opportunity to be a business angel and help aspiring entrepreneurs develop their ideas. It's so rewarding to be able to share my experience and empower others to achieve their own greatness.

Having the right mentors helps us sculpt a great idea into a fully realized business model. When we are committed to our vision and we demonstrate a passion to succeed, we inspire others to transmit the wisdom of their experience. When I was starting out as an entrepreneur, I decided to reach out to an author I respected and ask for his advice. Everyone told me, "Come on. He's not going to write back to you." Not only did he write back to me, he became someone I was able to go to for guidance.

Every aspiring entrepreneur should seek out three mentors who are experts in the fundamental aspects of any business:

- Creativity and Production
- Finance and Accounting
- Marketing and Communication

Surrounding ourselves with experienced people in our industry who can challenge our ideas and strategy helps us grow as leaders and makes our business plan stronger.

When I began building Mayshad, I knew I had a strong creative vision for the company, but I also had the humility to analyze what makes a business successful. Without a financial or marketing background, even the most creative idea can stagnate. To be a successful entrepreneur, I needed to be more than creative. Part of my mission became to educate myself in those areas where I was weakest. I immersed myself in circles where I could connect with people who had knowledge and experience in my field. I developed my communication skills and supported the company with financial experts. Now, I am entering a new phase as an entrepreneur where I am the creative director of my company, but I also have the experience and expertise to handle our finances and give voice to our vision.

THE LITTLE FROG

As leaders, we must have the humility to question our strategy, but we must also have the conviction and clarity of purpose to make our own decisions and not allow other people's doubts to influence our judgment.

Very early on in my journey as an entrepreneur, a good friend shared an inspirational story with me that I have never forgotten:

> *There was once a group of little frogs who got together and decided to have a race to the top of the highest tower in town. As news of the race spread, a large crowd of supporters began to gather around the tower. The moment the race began, the people standing on the sidelines began to worry for the little frogs.*
>
> *"Poor little frogs," they cried. "They're never going to make it!"*
>
> *As the race continued, many of the frogs grew tired, and some of them began to collapse and give up.*
>
> *"Poor little frogs," the spectators cried out. "Look at them. They're falling. They're never going to make it!"*

But, the race continued as the frogs that still had the strength passionately continued to climb higher and higher.

"They will never succeed!" one supporter cried out. "The tower is too high!"

"No, they will never make it to the top," another added. "It's way too difficult!"

One by one, the little frogs grew tired and gave up. One by one, they fell. Until, finally, there was only one little frog left.

"Poor little frog," the spectators all cried. "She's going to fall! She's never going to make it."

But, the little frog kept going, climbing higher and higher and higher. When she finally reached the top of the tower, all the supporters rushed to congratulate her for winning the race.

"Little frog, how did you do it?" they asked. "How did you make it to the top of the tower when all the other frogs failed?"

That's when they found out that the little frog was deaf.

This story of the little frog has been very important in my life. It makes me smile every time I share it because it came to me at a point when I needed to learn to embrace my vision, to stop listening to other people's doubts and negativity, and just jump with both feet into my life mission and the company that I was building for my daughters.

There's a reason spectators sit out on the sidelines. People who are not entrepreneurs don't have that capacity to judge because they don't understand what it takes to be in the race. The people closest to us (our families, for example) look at the risks we're taking and worry for us. They think they're being supportive, but, in reality, they are pointing out obstacles without offering solutions. They're passing on a stress that is related to their own experience. As entrepreneurs, we must guard our vision against the negative influence of doubters. We must be that little frog that is deaf to the naysayers and keep climbing higher and higher.

ENTREPRENEURIAL LEADERSHIP

Throughout this journey, we have been learning how to apply leadership principals to our lives. We have detached ourselves from our egos and worked on our inner selves. We have created a healthy ecosystem and lifestyle for our three bodies. And, we have projected a detailed vision of our future.

Transforming a vision into an action plan comes with knowing where we want to be in five years and building the right strategy to get our business there. Think of obstacles or challenges to that strategy as opportunities for growth and learning. As entrepreneurs, we cannot afford to stay down when we fall. Maintaining a healthy lifestyle that aligns our bodies, minds, and souls gives us the strength and positive energy that will drive us forward with determination.

An entrepreneur can hardly grow a business alone, so we must surround ourselves with a motivated team that is unified by our vision and energized by our ambition. Entrepreneurship is not just about providing a service or product. It's about empowering the people who work for us and inspiring them to strive for their own greatness.

The goal of the entrepreneur is success, and leadership is the fuel that drives us there. Having a vision and action plan allows us to stop living between the lines and draw our own. When we stop dreaming of greatness and dare to live it, we don't just rise to our potential, we inspire others to embrace their own.

So go forward fearlessly and Be Who You Want to Be.

ABOUT THE AUTHOR

Nezha Alaoui empowers women and young individuals to develop into strong, inspiring leaders through a number of successful initiatives. Her publications, exhibitions, and design collections have all reinforced her objective to be a "global advocate for change."

Through her missions for the United Nations working with the World Food Program under Ban Ki Moon mandate in Mozambique, Ethiopia, Senegal, Mauritania and Haiti in 2011, Nezha has developed a special understanding and close relationship with marginalized communities, especially youth and women in the third world. These experiences inspired her to create the Mayshad Foundation. The Foundation exists to strengthen marginalized communities through education, entrepreneurship, and sustainable solutions to climate change.

The US-based organization has been operating in Africa and focuses on implementing programs that offer solutions for meeting the 17 Sustainable Development Goals ("SDGs") adopted in 2015 by the United Nations in 193 countries and eight major groups with a special focus on vulnerable women and youth.

Nezha is a tireless and vocal advocate for these communities, amplifying their voice to address their often-overlooked needs. She is a consistent participant in conferences and panels throughout the world, spreading the word on the causes she supports.

Through the Mayshad Foundation, Nezha hosts conferences and events which bring together policymakers and other leaders to build awareness of and create actionable strategies to improve the lives of those in marginalized communities.